CIRCULAR WALKS
AROUND BEDDGELERT

CIRCULAR WALKS
AROUND
BEDDGELERT

Dorothy Hamilton

First edition: 2006
New edition: 2007
© Text: Dorothy Hamilton

ISBN: 1-84524-078-2
978-1-84524-078-3

Cover design: Alan Jones
Cover illustration: Dorothy Hamilton

First published in 2006 by Gwasg Carreg Gwalch
12 Iard yr Orsaf, Llanrwst, Wales LL26 0EH
℡ 01492 642031 📠 01492 641502
✆ books@carreg-gwalch.co.uk   Web site: www.carreg-gwalch.co.uk

New edition published in 2007 by Llygad Gwalch,
Ysgubor Plas, Llwyndyrys, Pwllheli, Gwynedd LL53 6NG
℡ 01758 750432 📠 01758 750438
✆ gai@llygadgwalch.com   Web site: www.carreg-gwalch.co.uk

Contents

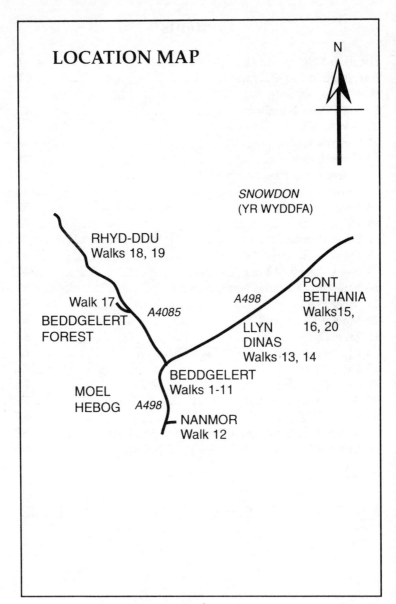

LOCATION MAP

N

SNOWDON
(YR WYDDFA)

RHYD-DDU
Walks 18, 19

PONT
BETHANIA
Walks15,
16, 20

Walk 17
BEDDGELERT
FOREST

A4085

A498

LLYN
DINAS
Walks 13, 14

BEDDGELERT
Walks 1-11

MOEL
HEBOG

A498

NANMOR
Walk 12

Introduction

Walks in this guide range from easy, fairly level walks, taking one or two hours, to all day mountain routes. The walks selected highlight the magnificent landscape and historical interest around Beddgelert.

All the walks have sketch maps and easy to follow directions. Walks 1-11 start from the main car park in Beddgelert whilst the others start from car parks within a few miles of the village. All are on, or near, bus routes.

Each route includes an introduction explaining the historical and legendary interest of the walk and places passed en route. The walks are graded according to length and terrain. Easy routes have low mileage and ascents are gentle or short. Moderate walks have longer uphill sections. The walks classed as strenuous include very steep sections or reach the mountain tops. The average time taken to complete each walk is given but extra time may be needed for food breaks, photography etc. Although adequate route directions are given to follow the walks without referring to other maps, it is advisable to carry the relevant maps on mountain routes. The Ordnance Survey 1:25 000 Explorer OL17 map covers the terrain of all the walks in this guide. It should be noted that some walks use permissive paths or cross open access land, and some of these paths are not shown on the Ordnance Survey map.

There are several cafes and restaurants in Beddgelert, but the majority of the walks do not pass refreshment places therefore, on the longer routes, it is advisable to carry some food and drink for snacks along the way. Almost all the walks require sturdy footwear and boots are recommended on the mountains. Take care – choose good weather for the high level walks and be prepared by carrying waterproofs and extra clothing.

Background

Beddgelert is a charming, small village nestling below mountains at the confluence of the rivers Afon Glaslyn and Afon Colwyn. The name means 'Gelert's Grave' and it may refer to a St Kelert, or Celer, an early Irish Christian missionary.

There was a Celtic Christian settlement here in the seventh century. It became well known for its hospitality and by the early 13th century a community of Augustinian canons called the Augustinian Priory of the Valley of the Blessed Mary of Snowdon was established. Fire damaged the priory in 1283, destroying ancient records, and it is significant that Edward I paid for it to be restored. There was another great fire in the 16th century and the priory was finally demolished at the time of the dissolution of the monasteries, during the reign of Henry VIII.

The land on the north side of the river had been given to the Cistercian Abbey of Aberconwy c. 1200 AD by Llywelyn ap Iorwerth. At that time, a farmhouse called Glasdraian stood where the present Saracen's Head Hotel is now. After the dissolution, the land was split up. The Augustinian priory lands were bought c. 1585 by John Wynn Morys and his family lived in the house now known as Bwthyn Llywelyn. The grave of one of his descendants can be seen in the churchyard.

By the late 18th century, tourists were visiting the area and a Mr Thomas Jones, whose wife had inherited the former priory lands, built the Beddgelert Hotel. Opened in 1802, its name was soon changed to the Goat Hotel, then The Royal Goat Hotel after the visit of Prince Arthur, Duke of Connaught. The first landlord, David Prichard, publicised the legend of the faithful hound Gelert and, it is said, he built the grave with the help of the parish clerk and another man.

By the time of the opening of the Beddgelert Hotel, there was an increasing demand for mountain guides. John Ray, the botanist, is thought to be the first person who hired a guide at Beddgelert. At that time, guides were usually hired at

Caernarfon. He lodged at 'Bethkellert' in September 1658 and hired a guide to take him up Yr Wyddfa. The mountain was covered in cloud but he found 'divers rare plants'. Much later, Richard Evans, the parish clerk who helped place the memorial slab on Gelert's Grave, was known as 'the father of all guides'. He lived in a house called Pen Bont Fach that stood near the present Prince Llywelyn Hotel. In St Mary's churchyard is the grave of Thomas Jones, a guide who moved to the village after marriage and lived in Church Street. He kept a diary, from which it is known he guided Lord Lewisham to the summit of Yr Wyddfa in 1846. The era of mountain guides ended in 1896 when the Snowdon Mountain railway started operating.

Before the boom in tourism, most people living near Beddgelert worked in agriculture but, by the late 18th century, several copper mines had opened. The miners earned more than farm workers but worked in appalling conditions for up to twelve hours a day, six days a week. Women also worked at the mines, breaking the ore. Some men lived in barracks but most walked from their homes each day. Remains of copper mining can be seen on some of the walks, especially in Cwm Bychan.

The copper was exported from Aber, a little port south of Pont Aberglaslyn. Tides came up almost as far as the bridge before William Alexander Madocks built his embankment at Porthmadog. There were turnpike roads passing through Beddgelert by the early 19th century and in 1923 the Welsh Highland Railway opened an extension of its line from Dinas – Rhyd-ddu to Beddgelert, Nanmor and Porthmadog. The track had to be cut through a long section of rock at Aberglaslyn Pass to reach Nanmor. It was built mainly for the purpose of transporting minerals from the slate quarries and copper mines which, it was hoped, would reopen. Many had closed prior to the coming of the railway because of transport difficulties. The trains also carried passengers, but the venture was not a success and stopped operating in 1937. For many years, it was possible to walk along the track and through the tunnels to Nanmor.

The tunnels have now been closed by the new Welsh Highland Railway, and work is in progress to restore the line to Porthmadog.

Much of the land around Beddgelert is now owned by the National Trust and, apart from their conservation work, the trust has created new footpaths, enabling walkers to explore even more of the beautiful countryside around Beddgelert.

Welsh Place-names

The following words are used in some of the place-names around Beddgelert.

Aber – *estuary, mouth*
Afon – *river*
Allt/Gallt – *hill*
Bach/Fach – *small*
Bedd – *grave, tomb*
Beudy – *cow shed*
Braich – *arm*
Bryn – *hill*
Bwlch – *pass*
Bychan – *little*
Cadair/Gadair – *chair*
Cae – *field*
Caer/Gaer – *fort*
Capel – *chapel*
Carreg – *stone*
Castell – *castle*
Cloch – *bell*
Clogwyn – *cliff, crag*
Coch – *red*
Coed – *wood, trees*
Craig – *rock*
Cwm – *valley*
Dinas – *fort*
Du/Ddu – *black*
Drws – *door*
Dyffryn – *valley, dale*
Eglwys – *church*
Ffordd – *road*
Ffridd – *mountain pasture*
Ffynnon – *spring, well*

Garn – *cairn*
Glan – *bank/shore*
Glas – *blue*
Hafod/Hafoty – *summer dwelling*
Hebog – *hawk, falcon*
Hen – *old*
Isaf – *lower*
Llan – *church*
Llyn – *lake*
Maen – *stone*
Maes – *field*
Mawr/Fawr – *big, great, large*
Melin – *mill*
Moel/Foel – *bare hill, mountain top*
Mor – *sea*
Muriau – *walls*
Mynydd/Fynydd – *mountain*
Nant – *brook, ravine*
Ogof – *cave*
Parc – *park, field*
Pen – *head, top*
Plas – *mansion*
Pont – *bridge*
Rhos – *moor*
Rhyd – *ford*
Tal – *tall, high*
Trwsgl – *awkward*
Tŷ – *house*
Uchaf – *upper*
Y/Yr – *the*

Useful Phone Numbers

Beddgelert Tourist Information Centre	01766 890615
Porthmadog Tourist Information Centre	01766 512981
Bws Gwynedd	01286 679535
Sygun Copper Mine	01766 510100
The National Trust (for Dinas Emrys)	01766 510120

WALK 1

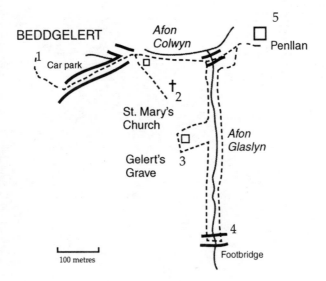

BEDDGELERT

Afon Colwyn

1 Car park

2 †

St. Mary's Church

Gelert's Grave

3

Afon Glaslyn

5

Penllan

4

Footbridge

100 metres

Gelert's Grave

Start: Beddgelert. Main car park off the A498.

Time: About 1 hour.

Grade: Easy.

Terrain: Pavements, lanes and (mainly) surfaced paths.

This easy, level, short walk leads you to some of the most interesting features in the village of Beddgelert.

On leaving the car park, at the main road, you will see to your right the Royal Goat Hotel. The original Beddgelert Hotel opened in 1802 and its first manager, David Prichard, promoted the local legend of Gelert to boost tourism in the village. A path (now nonexistent) led from the hotel to the grave.

Near the bridge, on the corner of Church Street, is Bwthyn Llywelyn, the oldest house in Beddgelert. Traditionally, it is believed to be on the site of the hunting lodge of Llywelyn ap Iorwerth – a renowned Welsh prince who was called Llywelyn Fawr (*Llywelyn the Great*). It was first called Y Priordy (*the priest's house*). It was a farmhouse in the 1580s but became a public house in the 18th century, offering accommodation to tourists. During a great flood in August 1799, when it was known as Ty Isaf, a man drowned inside the building. The inn was known for its two quart tankard, called 'Yr Hen Beint Mawr'. If a drinker could hold the tankard in one hand, with the other hand behind his back, and drink all the contents in one go, the beer would be paid for by the lord of the manor. During the early years of the 20th century, the building served as a tea room and accommodated cyclists. The National Trust bought it in 1985.

A short stroll down Church street leads to St Mary's Church.

Early Celtic Christians established a community in Beddgelert in the 7th century and in the early 13th century it became an Augustinian Priory. During the dissolution of the monasteries, between 1536 and 1539, the priory was dismantled and only the chapel was left standing to serve as the parish church. All that remains of the original chapel is the triple lancet east window and two arches. During the Victorian period, the church was considerably altered.

Some interesting graves are to be found in the churchyard. The oldest, under the yew tree near the entrance, is that of Ellis Wynne who died in 1672. On the other side of the path is the grave of Thomas Jones (1788-1877), who guided Victorian tourists up Snowdon. In the new cemetery, which is on the site of the former priory's buildings, is the grave of Edith Evans, 'Telynores Eryri' (1896-1984). There is an engraved harp on her gravestone (see Walk 2). Richard Griffiths, known as Carneddog (1862-1947) is also buried here. Coins from the reign of Henry III were found near the church porch when a grave was being dug in 1853.

Hotel manager David Prichard haunted the village after his death, until farm labourer Hwlyn followed him one day to the church porch and asked him why he kept wandering about. The ghost replied that he could not rest in his grave because of some money hidden in the bar room. He asked Hwlyn to tell Alice (his widow) to lift up the hearthstone, and there she would find two hundred guineas, two of which should be given to Hwlyn. Hwlyn delivered the message and the money was found.

Hailing from southern Wales, David Prichard claimed he had found Gelert's grave in the field opposite the hotel. He promoted the tragic tale and it brought in many tourists. The legend tells of Llywelyn Fawr who used to hunt around Beddgelert. One day, when he returned from hunting, he was met by his faithful hound covered in blood. In the lodge, he found more blood and an overturned cradle. Llywelyn assumed Gelert had killed the child and, in anger, plunged his sword into Gelert's side. Seconds too late, he heard the baby cry. Under the cot's bedding, he found his son, safe and well, next to the body of a dead wolf. Gelert had killed the wolf to save his master's baby. Full of remorse, Llywelyn buried him and marked his grave with a large stone.

A short diversion leads to the home of Alfred Bestall, the illustrator of Rupert Bear. He bought a cottage at Beddgelert in 1956 and visited the village several times a year. From 1980 it was his main home. The small cottage is called Penlan, the name of a house at Trefriw in Dyffryn Conwy (*dyffryn:* valley) where he stayed on holiday with his parents during the summers of 1912 and 1913. His father was a missionary and Alfred was born in Burma in 1892. At first educated in England, he then attended Rydal public school at Colwyn Bay in 1904. His first drawings appeared in *Blighty* and *Punch*. Mary Tourtel had created Rupert in 1920 but, in 1935, because of failing eyesight, she wanted someone else to take over. Alfred Bestall's first story in the *Daily Express* began on 28 December 1935, and the last story in the newspaper ended on 22 July 1965. His work also appeared in annuals and storybooks. Many of his illustrations were inspired by Beddgelert's surroundings. He loved children but never had any of his own. His 90th birthday, on 14 December 1982, was celebrated at a party given by the Girl Guides in Beddgelert. He died of bone cancer in January 1986, only nine days after becoming a resident of Wern Manor Nursing home, near Porthmadog.

Walk Directions:

1. From the car park, walk out to the A498 and turn left. Do not cross the bridge over Afon Colwyn, but turn right on a lane, passing Bwthyn Llywelyn (*bwthyn:* cottage) on your left. Walk along Church Street to St Mary's Church.

2. After visiting the church, return to the bridge and turn right to have the river on your left. Look out for a plaque on your right commemorating the filming of 'The Inn of the Sixth Happiness' in the area during the 1950s. It starred Ingrid Bergman. On reaching a footbridge, do not cross it, but turn right through a gate. With Afon Glaslyn now on your left, follow the riverside path until a sign directs you to Gelert's Grave.

3. From the grave, continue on a path to a building. Inside is a sculpture of Gelert. Ignore a gate and follow the path to the river and turn right. Continue along the path and go through another gate to a footbridge over Afon Glaslyn.

4. After crossing the bridge, bear left on a path to return along the opposite side of the river. At a picnic area on your right, walk along the embankment to a lane. Turn left and, at a junction, bear right. Penlan, Alfred Bestall's home is a short distance to your left (please do not enter the garden, it is private property).

5. Return to the junction and turn left. In a few paces, bear right on a path across the Green to the confluence of the rivers Glaslyn and Colwyn. Cross the footbridge to retrace your steps to the start.

Cwm Cloch

Start: Beddgelert. Main car park off the A498.

Time: About 1 hour.

Grade: Easy.

Terrain: Field paths, track and pavement. One short, easy
             uphill section.

This short, easy walk takes you very quickly away from the bustle of Beddgelert and, after a small height gain, offers fine views of the valley and Moel Hebog, as well as more distant hills and mountains.

On the walk you will pass Cwm Cloch Ganol, birthplace of Edith Evans (1896-1984), the famous Snowdonia harpist known as 'Telynores Eryri'. She established the Snowdonia Harp Choir in 1930. The members included her sister Ellen Ann Hughes and Nansi Richards (Telynores Maldwyn). Her home, Eryri Wen, in Beddgelert became well known for its beautiful, colourful gardens.

Opposite Beddgelert bridge, which you cross, stands the Prince Llywelyn Hotel. A Snowdon mountain guide called Richard Edwards and known as 'the father of guides' lived in a house called Pen Bont Fach near the site of the present hotel. Involved in the placing of the memorial to Gelert (see Walk 1), he died in March 1845, aged 74. In September 1949, a meteorite weighing over 700 grams plummeted through the roof of the hotel.

Walk Directions:

1. From the car park, walk out to the A498 and turn right. In a few paces, turn right to pass the Royal Goat Hotel on your left.

WALK 2

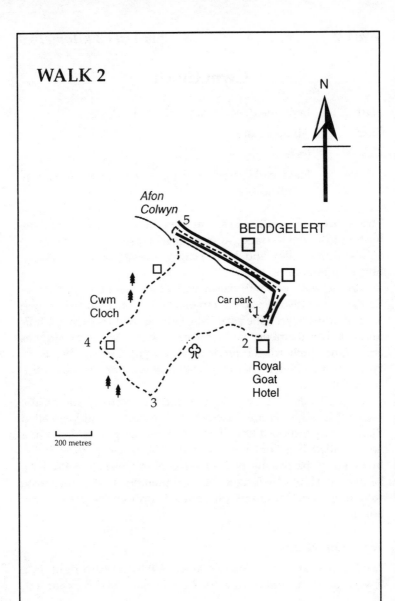

N

Afon Colwyn

5

BEDDGELERT

Cwm Cloch

Car park

1

4

2

3

Royal Goat Hotel

200 metres

When the road bends to the left, turn right on a track and, in a few metres, bear left on a footpath. Cross a road at houses and walk ahead to cross a bridge over the Welsh Highland Railway cutting.

2. Walk ahead through the field and pass through a gap into the next field. Go ahead to soon have a wall on your right and a marshy area to your left. In the far right-hand corner of the field, go through a small gate (or climb the ladder stile). Keep to the left side of this field at first, then head uphill to go through a gap. Go slightly left to a fence corner and follow the fence uphill. Pass a wood and gate on your left and a fenced area on your right. Keep on walking uphill and go through a gate onto a track. In front of you is Moel Hebog.

3. Bear right along the track and pass the edge of a plantation on your left. Further on, after passing old farm buildings and crossing a bridge, the track bends right at houses. The last house on your right has a plaque on the north facing wall commemorating the birth of the harpist Edith Evans.

4. Follow the track downhill. It goes through a plantation of pines and passes a farmhouse and farm buildings. After having a stream on your right for a short distance, go left with the track to pass under a bridge of the Welsh Highland Railway. Go through a small gate at a cattle grid and cross Pont Alun over Afon Colwyn.

5. Turn right along the pavement. A few metres after passing Y Warws (an Outdoor shop) on your right, you will see the drive to Eryri Wen (Edith Evan's home) on your left. Continue along the road, past the Saracen's Head Hotel, to the bridge. On your left is the Prince Llywelyn Hotel. Cross the bridge and turn right to return to the car park.

N

BEDDGELERT

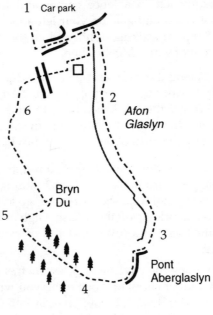

1 Car park

2 *Afon Glaslyn*

6

Bryn Du

5

3

Pont Aberglaslyn

4

500 metres

Aberglaslyn Pass and Bryn Du

Start: Beddgelert. Main car park off the A498.

Time: About 3 hours.

Grade: Moderate.

Terrain: Riverside path, great care needed in places especially with children (gorge section inadvisable when the river is high), steep woodland path, hillside and field paths.

On this walk you follow a rocky riverside path, known as the Fisherman's Path, through the dramatic Aberglaslyn gorge. At the narrowest part of the ravine, the road, river and path are hemmed in on both sides by 700 foot high, precipitous hillsides. After reaching Aberglaslyn bridge, the route then climbs through National Trust owned woodlands to an open hillside with panoramic views of the valley and surrounding mountains.

The old Welsh name for Aberglaslyn Pass is 'Y Gymwynas', meaning *'The Favour'*. Perhaps it was called this because it linked Beddgelert with the sea, and in the olden days most trade came by sea. A bridle path led through the gorge before the road was built. In the 18th and 19th centuries, the pass attracted many artists and writers. Thomas Pennant, in his *Tour of Wales*, speaks of the scenery as the most magnificent that can be imagined.

Before the building of the embankment at Porthmadog, numerous salmon came up the river to spawn. It is thought that Llywelyn ap Iorwerth owned a fishery in the pass, and at one time the weirs belonged to the English crown. Travellers amused themselves by watching the salmon attempting to leap over the rocks and weirs.

Until the early 19th century when the sands were drained, tides came within a short distance of Aberglaslyn bridge. Ships laden with various goods sailed as far as Aberglaslyn village, sited at the highest navigable point of the river. It was there that people from the parish of Beddgelert did their trading. Copper ore from the nearby mines was exported from the little port and small coasters were built on the sands. In the mid 18th century, the village contained about 15 houses and a tavern called Y Delyn *(The Harp)*. Nothing remains of the village now,

In Coed Aberglaslyn and on the walk down Bryn Du, you will notice ruined buildings associated with the copper industry. Copper ore was mined intermittently in this area from the 18th century until the 1870s.

Walk Directions:

1. From the car park, walk out to the A498 and turn left. Do not cross the bridge over Afon Colwyn but go ahead on a lane beside the river. Cross the footbridge over Afon Glaslyn and immediately bear right to have the river on your right. High above on your left is Craig y Llan.

2. Pass a footbridge over Afon Glaslyn and continue along the old trackbed of the Welsh Highland Railway. (If the new railway line is in place, there should be a crossing to a path beside the river.) Leave the trackbed after about 300 metres, when the river is close by, and go right on a path to walk along the riverbank. A narrow path takes you around a buttress (there are handholds) directly above the river as you enter the narrowest part of the gorge. Continue on the rocky path, with a little scrambling here and there, until you meet the road at Pont Aberglaslyn.

3. Go out onto the road and cross the bridge. Turn left on the A498 (take care) and, in about 100 metres, bear right on a path.

It is not very conspicuous, but is close to a Beddgelert sign. There is a National Trust Coed Aberglaslyn sign near the path. Cross a stile and walk on beside the right-hand fence. After about 100 metres, when the path forks, bear right through a small gate.

4. Follow the steep path uphill through the woodlands. There are steps in places and arrows to guide you. Higher up, the path goes through a wall to more steps and small log bridges over drainage channels. Eventually, you leave the trees by climbing a ladder stile over a high wall.

5. The path continues through heather and bracken with superb views all around. Go ahead to a small tower, a good viewpoint, then take the descending path through a boggy area. Further downhill, it passes through a small gate at a left-hand fence corner. Pass a ruin on your right and cross a ladder stile. Continue along the left side of a field.

6. Go through a small gate and walk ahead through gorse and bracken. The path veers right to gates at the A498. Cross the road to more gates and go ahead on a track but, when it bears right, go ahead to a small gate. Join a concrete path and bear left along it for a few paces to Gelert's Grave. Keep ahead to a gate then turn right to the riverbank. Go left to the footbridge at the confluence of the rivers Glaslyn and Colwyn, then retrace your steps to the start of the walk.

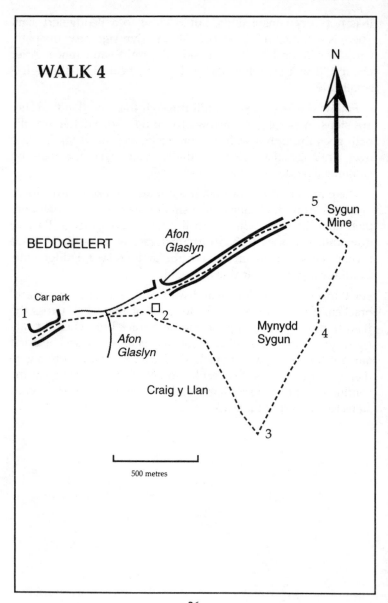

WALK 4

N

Sygun
Mine

5

BEDDGELERT

Afon
Glaslyn

Car park

1

2

Afon
Glaslyn

Mynydd
Sygun

4

Craig y Llan

3

500 metres

Craig y Llan

Start: Beddgelert. Main car park off the A498.

Time: 2-3 hours.

Grade: Moderate/Strenuous.

Terrain: Very steep, partly rocky climb at the start to a height of 1000 feet. This is followed by easier hill paths, a quiet lane and a short stretch of riverside path.

The steep hill that overlooks Beddgelert from the south-east is known as Craig y Llan. Although only 1000 feet high, this little mountain offers extensive views over the surrounding countryside. From its summit, the panorama includes Moel Hebog, Moel yr Ogof, Moel Lefn, the Nantlle range and, continuing clockwise, Yr Aran with Yr Wyddfa *(Snowdon)* behind. Nearer peaks are Moel y Dyniewyd, Y Cnicht and the Moelwyn mountains. To the south lies the Glaslyn estuary.

The walk continues over Mynydd Sygun and descends through rhododendrons to the Sygun Copper Mine, now a tourist attraction. A typical copper mine, Sygun was worked in the 18th and 19th centuries, finally closing in 1903. After some renovation work, it opened to the public in 1986.

The mining started high on the hillside, where the ore veins outcropped near the surface, and then followed the main lode deep into the mountain. The lower levels had to be drained by bucket and hand pumps. Miners worked by candle light, using hand tools. A common practice was to take bracken into the mine to provide a dry place for rest and meals. Work was by contract and the average miner earned between £1 and £2 each month for a ten hour, six day week.

In 1958, the land near Sygun Mine Visitor Centre was transformed into a Chinese village, complete with pagodas and houses for the making of the film 'The Inn of the Sixth Happiness' starring Ingrid Bergman, Curt Jurgens and Robert Donat.

Walk Directions:

1. From the car park, walk out to the A498 and turn left to the bridge. Do not cross the bridge but take a lane to have the river on your left. Cross the footbridge over Afon Glaslyn and take a path that crosses the Green, away from the river. Bear left on a lane and, in a few metres, turn right at a junction. A cottage on your left called Penlan was the home of Alfred Bestall, illustrator of the Rupert Bear stories.

2. At the end of the lane, go through a kissing-gate to the start of the steep climb up Craig y Llan. A few minutes scrambling up the rocky path brings you to a grassy viewpoint over Beddgelert. Pause for breath, then continue upwards to the right over rocks and, eventually, you will reach a kissing-gate in a wall. After going through the gate, take a path to the right. It climbs through rocks, rhododendrons and heather to a craggy viewpoint. Go ahead across fairly level ground to the summit of Craig y Llan on its little ridge.

3. Walk south-west a few paces along the ridge then bear left on a path that passes below the highest point. The path soon levels out for a while and has rocky outcrops to the right. After a short descent, and just before reaching a marshy area, bear right on a path through heather to a cairn. Pass the cairn on your left and, maintaining your direction, take a path just below the ridge, ignoring paths to the left and right. Further on, follow the path up to the ridge and keep ahead until you reach another cairn. Here, take a path on the left side of the ridge ahead and pass a signpost for Beddgelert and Sygun. In a few more metres, you will reach a path junction.

4. Turn left downhill on a path that soon becomes stony and passes through rhododendrons to emerge at a viewpoint near the exit of Sygun Copper Mine. Continue ahead on the track and follow it to the left downhill. Follow a fence on your right to a track near the entrance to the mine.

5. Turn left on the track and go through a gate onto a lane. Continue ahead for just over one kilometre and, where the lane bends right to cross a bridge over Afon Glaslyn, climb a stile in the wall on your left. With the river on your right, follow the path through rhododendrons to a little gate and walk ahead to the next gate. Cross over a lane to a path and, in a few metres, you will emerge at the Green in Beddgelert. Cross the footbridge over Afon Glaslyn to retrace your steps to the start of the walk.

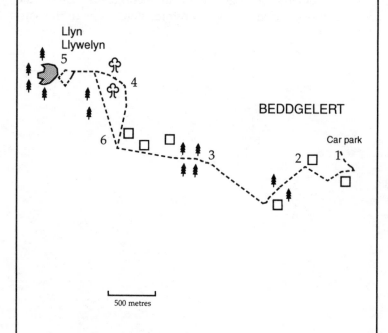

WALK 5

N

Llyn
Llywelyn

5

4

BEDDGELERT

Car park

6

3

2

1

500 metres

Llyn Llywelyn

Start: Beddgelert. Main car park off the A498.

Time: 3-4 hours.

Grade: Moderate.

Terrain: Rough field paths and forest tracks.

This very, pleasant walk wanders along forest tracks to a beautiful, small, tree encircled lake lying beneath the crags of Moel Lefn. This atmospheric spot makes a fine place for a picnic.

According to legend, the hollow containing Llyn Llywelyn was formed by a giant who jumped into the cwm from a rock called Llam Trwsgl in the Colwyn valley, while taking part in a jumping competition with another giant.

Large areas of Beddgelert forest have been felled, opening up magnificent views of the Snowdon range. The Forestry Commission planted the first coniferous trees in the forest at Pont Cae'r Gors in 1926.

On the walk, you pass above Meillionen farmhouse. In the 18th century two bachelors lived here and, one evening, they received a visitor from Anglesey who claimed to have a reoccurring dream directing him to treasure buried under a stone at a ruin called Hafod Ernallt on the land of Meillionen. The crafty bachelors told him there was a farm called Meillionydd on the Llŷn peninsula and, early the next morning, they guided him over Bwlch Cwm Trwsgl to set him on his way. Immediately afterwards, they went to the ruin of Hafod Ernallt, located only about 500 metres from Meillionen, and found a pitcher underneath a stone. It is said the contents of gold and silver weighed over sixty pounds. Hafod Ernallt was probably medieval and one of its rooms had no doors or windows, with only a small hole for entry.

Walk Directions:

1. Walk out of the car park to the A498 and turn right. Almost immediately, bear right to pass the Royal Goat Hotel on your left. When this road bends left, turn right on a track and, in a few paces, take a path on your left. Cross over an access road at houses, and keep ahead to cross a footbridge over the Welsh Highland Railway track. Turn right on a grassy track between walls and veer left above a stream to a ladder stile. Cross a bridge and turn left on a lane.

2. Pass farm buildings on your right and follow the lane through pines to more buildings. Immediately after passing a barn on your right, climb a stile on your right and follow the path ahead for about 100 metres, then bear right to go through a gate in a wall. Turn left and cross the top of a drainage ditch, then continue beside the left-hand wall to a small gate. Cross another channel and pass through some trees to reach another gate. Cross a stream, then climb a stile and walk uphill to a forest track.

3. Turn left to walk uphill and ignore paths and tracks leading off. Further on, there are open views as the track passes above Meillionen Farm and a barn. Cross a bridge and in a few metres, at a track junction, turn right downhill. Ignore a track on the right to a house and, further downhill, join another track. Turn left and ignore a track to Beddgelert Bikes but, after about another 100 metres, turn left on an old forest road.

4. Walk uphill through deciduous trees and cross over a track. Continue uphill and keep ahead at another junction of tracks. In about 100 metres, you will reach a picnic area at Llyn Llywelyn.

5. Turn left beside the lake and cross a bridge over the stream. Join a track and turn left to the crossroads of tracks reached

earlier. Bear right to retrace your steps downhill to the next track crossroads and turn right. The track soon starts to descend and wide views open up. Ignore a track on the right and one on the left and continue along the main track to rejoin your outward route just before a bridge.

6. Continue above the fields and Meillionen Farm, then pass through the forest to a left-bend in the track. Here go right on a path to the stile and stream crossed earlier. Retrace your steps to the start.

WALK 6

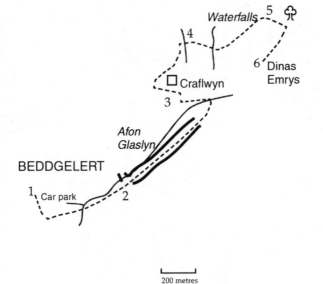

N

Waterfalls

5

6 Dinas Emrys

4

□ Craflwyn

3

Afon Glaslyn

BEDDGELERT

1 Car park

2

200 metres

Dinas Emrys

Start: Beddgelert. Main car park off the A498.

Time: About 3 hours.

Grade: Moderate.

Terrain: Lane, field, woodland and ridge paths.

Please note – Dinas Emrys is a fragile site and you are advised to contact the National Trust at Craflwyn before starting out on your walk. (See the list of phone numbers.)

Dinas Emrys is a small, rocky hill lying between Beddgelert and Llyn Dinas. According to legend it is the site of an ancient fortress established by Vortigern (Gwrtheyrn), a 5th century British king who had asked the Saxons to help him defend his kingdom in south-east England. He retreated to Gwynedd after they ousted him from his own lands. His magicians found him a site in Gwynedd on which to build his fortress but, every night, the walls collapsed. After more consultations, his advisors told him that he needed to find a fatherless boy. If such a boy was killed and his blood sprinkled on the rocks, the spell would be broken.

Eventually, after a long search, a boy who had no earthly father was found. His name was Myrddin Emrys (Ambrosius) but, on being brought to the fortress, he asked the reason for his fate. He told Vortigern that his magicians were fools and he, Myrddin (Merlin), could show him why the castle did not stand. Underneath the foundations of the castle, there was a lake and a red dragon and a white dragon. Every night, the dragons woke up and fought each other for the possession of a white cloth and the tremors from their battles caused the fortress to collapse.

The lake and the dragons were found and, on awakening, they fought for the white cloth. At first, the white dragon seemed the stronger, but the red dragon gained ground and chased the white dragon away. Myrddin explained to Vortigern that the red dragon represented the Celtic people and the white dragon, the Saxons. The result of the battle showed that the Celtic people would eventually prevail over the Saxons. The red dragon, of course, is the emblem of Wales.

The magicians were executed and buried in a field between Dinas Emrys and Craflwyn. Vortigern went to Nant Gwrtheryn on the Llŷn peninsula and Myrddin took possession of the castle. Eventually, he too had to leave, but left behind a hidden hoard of treasure including a golden throne. It is said if anyone searches for it, and they are not destined to find it, there will be a ferocious thunderstorm.

Excavations in the 1950s revealed that the site had been occupied in the late Roman period and also in the 5th century, the time of Vortigern. Finds included pieces of 5th century pottery.

The western ramparts remain and a little of the walls on the north and south sides. In the centre of the site, there is a pool and the footings of a tower (possibly 13th century) stands above it.

Walk Directions:

1. From the car park, go out to the A498 and turn left. Do not cross the bridge, but go ahead on a lane, with the river on your left. Cross the footbridge over Afon Glaslyn and take the path on the left beside the river, passing the Green on your right. Cross over a lane and go through a kissing-gate to a footpath and, at the next bridge, climb a stile onto a lane.

2. Bear right along the lane and, at its end, go through a gate onto a track. Immediately, bear left on a path through bracken and have a wall on your left. Emerge on another track (Sygun Copper Mine is to your right) and turn left. Ignore a path on

your right (it leads to Llyn Dinas) and cross a bridge over the river to the road. Go through a small gate on your left and walk on beside the river, crossing small footbridges over streams. At steps, go up to the road and cross, slightly right (take care), to the entrance gates of Craflwyn Hall.

3 Follow the drive and bear left to a fork. Turn right uphill to pass between buildings and the back of Craflwyn Hall. Go through a gate and, in about 50 metres, ignore a path on the left (this is the route of Walk 14). Have a wall on your left and, in about another 80 metres, look for a green arrow (National Trust), where you bear left to a small gate. Walk on beside a wall and go through a gap to cross a footbridge on your right. Climb a ladder stile in the right-hand wall and go ahead through bracken, with rocky outcrops to your left. Go through a wall gap and descend through trees to a wall. Have a small waterfall on your left and, in a few paces, cross a bridge over the stream.

4. Walk on with the stream on your right. The path veers left to have a wall on the right as you pass above a field. Further right is the hill of Dinas Emrys. On reaching a wall corner, ignore the path going uphill, but continue beside the right-hand wall.

5. Cross a ladder stile into woodlands and go slightly left uphill, passing rocky outcrops. Keep ahead on the path until you have a fence on the right. Cross a small stile in it and go ahead on a clear path. It passes through a gap in the rocks and veers to the right along a ridge, passing through bracken and over rocks. Take care as there are steep drops to your left. After a short, easy scramble, you will soon reach the highest point and the ancient fort of Dinas Emrys.

6. From Dinas Emrys, retrace your steps to the start as it is not possible to make this into a circular route. You could extend your walk by taking the path to Llyn Dinas from the bridge at the entrance to Sygun Mine. Alternatively, you could join Walk 14 above Craflwyn Hall, but this would make a very long day.

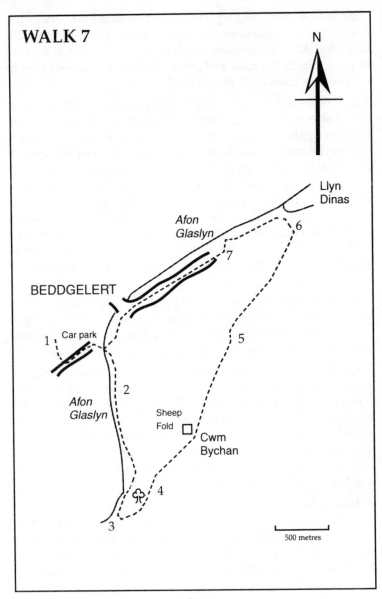

WALK 7

N

Llyn Dinas

Afon Glaslyn

7

BEDDGELERT

6

Car park

1

5

2

Afon Glaslyn

Sheep Fold

Cwm Bychan

4

3

500 metres

Walk 7   *6 miles/9.8 kilome*

Cwm Bychan

Start: Beddgelert. Main car park off the A498.

Time: 3-4 hours.

Grade: Moderate.

Terrain: Riverside paths (care needed), hill paths and lane.

After following the rocky Fisherman's Path beside Afon Glaslyn, the walk climbs up through Cwm Bychan with its copper mining remains before dropping down to Llyn Dinas and an easy level walk back to Beddgelert.

The Cwm Bychan copper mines were at their busiest between 1782 and 1802. From then onwards they were worked intermittently until the 1930s. On the walk, you will pass several pylons, the remains of an aerial ropeway from the 1920s that carried the copper ore from the mines to a processing plant at the lower end of the valley, near the Welsh Highland Railway track. Apparently, the system did not work very well and the buckets often hit the ground, spilling the ore. Other visible remains from the copper mining era are spoil heaps, adits and ruined buildings.

Walk Directions:

1. From the car park, walk out to the main road and turn left. Do not cross the bridge over Afon Colwyn, but walk ahead on a lane beside the river. At the confluence with Afon Glaslyn, cross the footbridge and bear right to have Afon Glaslyn on your right.

2. After passing a footbridge over the river you walk along the old trackbed of the Welsh Highland Railway. (If the new

railway line has arrived, there should be a crossing for you to continue beside the river.) Leave the trackbed after about 300 metres, when the river is closeby, and take a path on the right along the riverbank. The path goes around a rock buttress (there are handholds) above the river as you enter the narrowest part of the gorge. Continue on the rocky path, with a little scrambling in places, to eventually climb up into woodland.

3. Just before reaching Pont Aberglaslyn and a lane, go left up steps and pass above a house. After going through two small gates, you will see the old railway tunnel on your left. (If the railway is now in use and there is no crossing then after the first gate take a path on the right to a stile and go ahead through a small gate under the railway bridge. Bear left to the higher path and turn right.) The path now climbs up through trees and, just before a gate, you will see a small waterfall on your right.

4. Walk ahead, uphill through Cwm Bychan and, after crossing a stream, pass a sheepfold on your left and, further on, spoil heaps and pylons. After the last pylon, keep walking ahead, and ignore paths to the left. Continue uphill to the gap in the hills.

5. Climb a stile and enjoy the views from the pass before descending left to a path junction at a footpath signpost. Ignore the path on your left (which passes the remains of the Llyndu copper mine) and continue downhill. After a fairly level stretch, the path becomes steeper and beautiful views open up of Llyn Dinas.

6. On reaching another path near the lakeside, go left through a kissing-gate. Ignore the footbridge on the right and follow the clear path ahead. Go through a small gate to pass below a house and, after another gate, go left on a track. Pass Sygun Mine car park on your left and go through a gap in a wall then, immediately, bear right on a grassy path. After joining another

track, bear right through a gate onto a lane.

7. Follow the lane for about a kilometre and, where the lane bends right to cross a bridge, climb a stile on the left. Continue beside the river, through rhododendrons, to a little gate. Further on, go through a kissing-gate, cross a lane, and follow the path to the Green near the footbridge over Afon Glaslyn. Retrace your steps to the start.

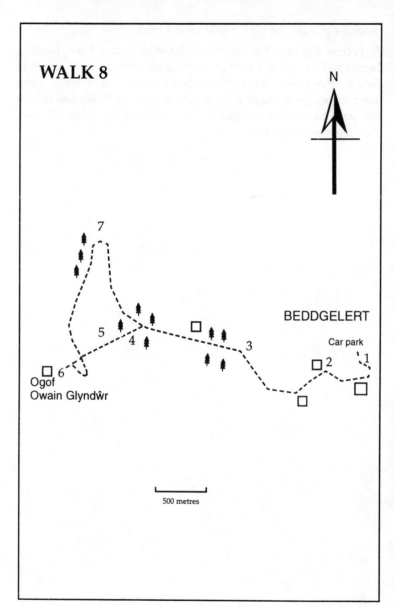

WALK 8

N

7

BEDDGELERT

Car park

5

4

3

1

2

6

Ogof
Owain Glyndŵr

500 metres

42

Owain Glyndŵr's Cave

Start: Beddgelert. Main car park off the A498.

Time: 4 hours

Grade: Moderate , with one strenuous climb.

Terrain: Rough field paths, forest tracks and paths. The
                walk includes a short, steep climb through an area
                of felled forest on a path unsuitable for young
                children.

This walk takes you to a viewpoint of the cave where,
reputedly, Owain Glyndŵr hid for several months after
escaping capture by King Henry IV's men. The route follows
forest paths and tracks with open views.

Owain Glyndŵr was born c.1359 in Dyffryn Dyfrdwy *(Dee
Valley)*. The beautiful court at Sycharth in the Tanat Valley was
the main family home. A descendant of the Princes of Powys
and Deheubarth, Owain was only ten years old when he
inherited the estate after his father's death. He studied law and
trained as a soldier, fighting for the crown in Scotland and
France.

After Edward I's huge and expensive armies ravaged Wales
and its people in the 13th century, the crown built a ring of
castles and colonial towns to secure an invader's foothold on
the verges of the Welsh mountain stronghold. Anti-Welsh laws
were passed and racial oppression followed and it was only a
matter of time before the Welsh raised in arms against the
foreign tyranny they were exposed to in their own country.

After Henry IV became king, there were disputes over land
claimed by Owain Glyndŵr and Lord Grey of Rhuthun.
Glyndŵr gathered his supporters at his home near Carrog in

Dyffryn Dyfrdwy and on 16 September 1400 (Fair Day), they attacked the castle and burnt the colonial town of Rhuthun. This was the start of a war of Welsh independence that lasted 15 years, during which Glyndŵr held parliament at Pennal and Machynlleth.

According to local legend, during a period of misfortune, Owain Glyndŵr sought refuge at Hafod Garegog, the house of Rhys Goch, a bard, near Nanmor. Eventually, his enemies learnt of his whereabouts and, one day, a servant of Rhys Goch saw soldiers with swords approaching Hafod Garegog. Owain and Rhys dressed themselves as servants and headed into the mountains. Rhys went in the direction of Nanmor and Owain headed towards the sea.

Owain's enemies soon caught sight of him and, with the soldiers in close pursuit, Owain swam across what is now Afon Glaslyn, (at that time the sea came as far as Aberglaslyn) and scrambled up Cwm Oerddwr to find himself below the precipices of Moel Hebog. There was no time to take the safe way up the mountain's shoulder and, in desperation because one slip would mean certain death, he climbed, by hand and foot, the three hundred foot cleft in the precipice called Simnai y Foel. King Henry's soldiers dared not follow him and took the easy route to the ridge, by which time Owain was nowhere in sight. They assumed he had descended to Cwm Pennant and searched for him there.

Glyndŵr, however, had followed the ridge over Moel Hebog and descended to the overhang (now known as Ogof Owain Glyndŵr) in the east face of Moel yr Ogof. He lived there for six months and, during that time, the Prior of Beddgelert brought him food.

Owain Glyndŵr survived to continue his revolt but his support gradually waned, and where he ended his days is unknown. But he had set out his vision for the future where Wales would have an independent church, two universities, a parliament and Welsh would be restored as an official language. He succeeded in maintaining his struggle for years against one of the richest nations in the world at that time. Although he never achieved permanent military victory, he kept his dream alive and subsequent generations inspired by him spent the next six hundred years trying to fulfil his objectives. He is considered to be the father of modern Wales, and his name and banner are seen throughout Wales today.

Walk Directions:

1. Walk out of the car park to the A498 and turn right, then right again to pass the Royal Goat Hotel on your left. When the road bends left, turn right on a track and, in a few paces, bear left on a path. Cross a road at houses and keep walking ahead to cross a footbridge over the Welsh Highland Railway track. Turn right on a track between walls and stay on it as it bears left to a ladder stile. Cross a bridge and bear left on a lane.

2. Pass farm buildings on your right and follow the track through a plantation to more buildings. Pass a barn on your right then, immediately, cross a stile on your right. Follow the obvious path for about 100 metres then bear right and go through a gate in a wall. Turn left and follow the wall to a small gate. Cross a channel and walk through some trees to a gate and stream. Climb the stile opposite and walk uphill to join a forest track on a bend.

3. Turn left and walk uphill, ignoring other paths and tracks leading off. Pass above Meillionen Farm and a barn. Cross a bridge and continue on the track for a few metres to where a track goes off to the right. Ignore this track, but leave the main track by taking a narrower one on the left.

4. On emerging at a track junction, turn left and, in about 150 metres, cross a bridge. In a few paces, just before the next bridge, bear right at a yellow arrow to follow a rough, steep path uphill through an area of felled forest. Higher up, it

crosses a stream on the left and continues rising until it emerges on a forest track.

5. Turn left for a few paces then take a path on the right to walk uphill over less steep ground and through rocks and heather with great views all around you. The path continues uphill over two more forest tracks to reach a turning point at the end of a track. If you continue uphill for a few metres, you will reach a stile and the open hillside. From here is a clear view of Owain Glyndŵr's cave on a ledge near the top of the cliff in front of you.

6. You may choose to retrace your steps to Beddgelert but, to vary your walk, go downhill from the stile to the forest track and follow it to the right, downhill. Ignore a track on the right at a left bend and the path you walked earlier. Further on, ignore a track on the left that goes uphill, and another on the right. Continue walking ahead, with rocky outcrops on your left, to reach a seat and a great viewpoint at a track junction. Turn left, downhill and, in about 400 metres, you will pass a footpath on your left.

7. After a few more paces, take a footpath on your right. It crosses a stream, and a track twice (to cut off a bend) to emerge on another track that offers superb views towards Snowdon. Turn right and ignore a track on the left and, further on, a track on the right at a clearing. Walk downhill to join your outward route near a bridge. Continue along the track above Meillionen Farm and further on, at the bend in the track, take the path on the right to retrace your steps to the start.

Pen y Gaer and Pont Aberglaslyn

Start: Beddgelert. Main car park off the A498.

Time: 4 hours.

Grade: Moderate/Strenuous.

Terrain: Rough hillside, woodland and riverside paths. Some paths may be boggy underfoot or indistinct on the ground. The walk is best taken during a spell of dry weather with good visibility.

You can enjoy some of the best views of the countryside around Beddgelert on this walk. From the moorland path above Aberglaslyn Pass, views extend to Yr Wyddfa *(Snowdon)*, Yr Aran, Moel Siabod, Y Cnicht and the Moelwyn mountains, so be sure to choose a clear day.

The route passes the remote farmhouse Oerddwr Uchaf, birthplace of William Francis Hughes, 'William Oerddwr', a local poet. Just beyond the house is the small Iron Age hill fort, Pen y Gaer. From the fort, the walk heads downhill to Pont Aberglaslyn. Before Porthmadog and its embankment were built, the tide came within a short distance of the bridge. The house beside it was originally a toll-gate house. Aberglaslyn once had 15 houses, but by the late 19th century only seven remained. The householders believed their land to be freehold and no one paid any rent. One day, a bailiff and three other men arrived and evicted the cottagers, demolishing their homes without any explanation.

From the bridge, the walk takes the rocky, Fisherman's Path to Beddgelert. An alternative, recommended if the river is high, is to follow the road until you can join a riverside path on the west bank.

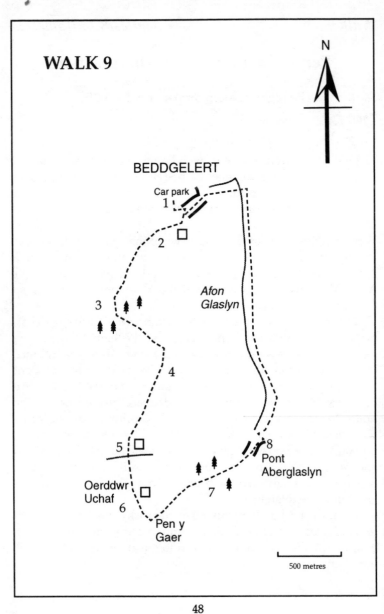

WALK 9

N

BEDDGELERT

Car park

1

2

Afon
Glaslyn

3

4

5

Oerddwr
Uchaf

6

Pen y
Gaer

7

8
Pont
Aberglaslyn

500 metres

Walk Directions:

1. From the car park, walk out to the road and turn right. After a few paces, bear right to pass the Royal Goat Hotel on your left. When the road curves left, bear right on a track and, in a few paces, turn left on a path. Cross a road at houses and go ahead to cross the footbridge over the Welsh Highland Railway track.

2. Continue straight ahead and, after going through a gap, have a wall on your right. Follow it to the far right-hand corner of the field and go through a gate (or climb the stile). Keep to the left and walk up the field to a gap in the wall. Head slightly left to a fence and follow it uphill, passing a fenced off area on your right. Emerge through a gate (be sure to look back at the views) and cross a track to another gate. Walk ahead, veering slightly left to pass a way marked post. Cross a drainage channel and keep angling to the left as you continue ahead. You will soon have a wall on your right.

3. Go through a gate at a gap in the plantation and head uphill, away from the trees. In about 200 metres, you should join another path that rises from the bottom of the hill. This point is roughly midway between the conifers and deciduous trees to your left. As the gradient eases, cross a low, overgrown wall that contours the hill. Bear left on a path (it may not be very clear) and follow it as it rises and rounds the hillside to give views of the Moelwynion and Y Cnicht.

4. The path goes through a gap in a wall, passes above a sheep pen, and goes through another gap to have a wall on the left. After about 50 metres, the path rises slightly above the wall and, ignoring a path on the right, follow it ahead. You will soon see a broad, flat area below. When the path curves to the right, go left downhill in the direction of a sheep pen. Pass it on your left and bear slightly left to pass around a small hill.

5. Cross a stream, Afon Goch, near a wall and continue ahead for a few metres to cross another stream. Veer left downhill and pass a rock face on your right. Go through a gap and continue beside a wall to pass through another gap. Walk through marshy ground and soon have a broken wall on your left. Follow the path to Oerddwr-Uchaf.

6. Pass the farmhouse on your left and continue along a track. Go through a gate across the track and, immediately, bear left to have a wall on your left. The small, rocky hill to your right is Pen y Gaer. Cross a stream and wall, then bear right to a gap. Have the wall on your left and, after it rounds a corner, continue downhill to pass a fenced enclosure to your right. After passing a sheepfold on your left, the path becomes clearer and heads downhill, with a stream and woods on the left, to a stile.

7. After entering the wood, follow the path between low, moss covered walls downhill through the trees. Eventually, the path bends right and, at a small gate, you turn left and cross a footbridge. Ignore a gate on the left and follow the path to the road. Turn left and, after about 100 metres, bear right to cross the bridge over Afon Glaslyn.

8. Turn left through a kissing-gate and ignore paths on the right. Walk ahead through the trees, following the path as it drops down to the river. The way ahead through Aberglaslyn gorge becomes rocky, and some scrambling is necessary here and there. After the path becomes easier, continue ahead with the river on your left, until you reach the confluence with Afon Colwyn near the Green. Turn left across the footbridge and follow the lane and road to your start in Beddgelert.

Blaen Nanmor and Nantgwynant

Start: Beddgelert. Main car park off the A498.

Time: 5 hours.

Grade: Moderate.

Terrain: Riverside path (take care), woodland and hillside paths, lanes.

This varied walk starts by following the Fisherman's Path through the Aberglaslyn Pass. It then traverses the woodlands of Nanmor and crosses low hills, with superb views of Yr Wyddfa *(Snowdon)*, to Llyn Dinas and a level, easy walk back to Beddgelert.

On the route you will pass Carneddi, once the home of Richard Griffith (Carneddog), a poet and writer whose grave is in Beddgelert churchyard. Hywel Gruffudd, one of his ancestors and also a bard, was born at Carneddi.

The area close to the river near Berthlwyd was a favourite meeting place for the people of Nanmor and Llyn Gwynant to hold games on the Sabbath before the non-conformist revival.

The walk passes close to Hafod Owen, the home of climber John Menlove Edwards from August 1941 to October 1942. A psychiatrist who was also a conscientious objector, he stayed in this isolated cottage whilst writing up his psychiatric research. He pioneered several hard climbing routes in Snowdonia and wrote a climbing guide with Wilfrid Noyce, a member of the 1953 Everest expedition. Menlove suffered from depression and in 1958, while living on the South Downs, he ended his life by swallowing potassium cyanide. His ashes were scattered from the wooded knoll above Hafod Owen.

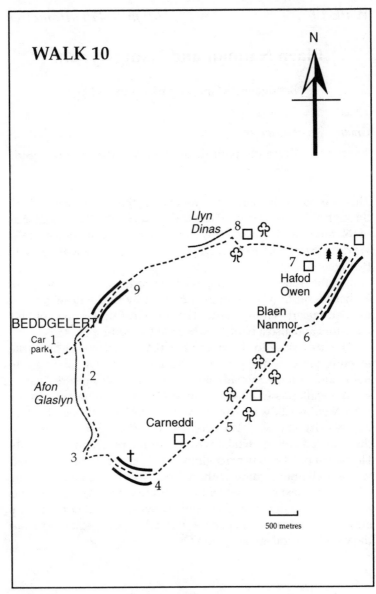

WALK 10

N

Llyn Dinas

BEDDGELERT

Car park

Afon Glaslyn

Carneddi

Hafod Owen

Blaen Nanmor

500 metres

Walk Directions:

1. From the car park, walk out to the A498 and turn left. Do not cross the bridge over Afon Glaslyn, but walk ahead on a lane beside the river. Cross the footbridge over Afon Glaslyn and, immediately, bear right on a path to have the river on your right.

2. Pass a footbridge spanning Afon Glaslyn and continue along the old trackbed of the Welsh Highland Railway. (If the new railway line is in place, there should be a crossing for you to be able to walk on beside the river.) Leave the trackbed after about 300 metres, when the river is closeby, and veer right on a path to walk along the riverbank. A narrow path takes you around a buttress (there are handholds) as you enter the narrowest part of the gorge. Continue on the rocky path until you reach a lane at Pont Aberglaslyn.

3. Just before the lane, go left on a path through the trees and walk above a house. After going through two small gates, you will see the old railway tunnel on your left. Turn right to follow the old railway track and, when you meet a lane, turn left. (If the railway line is in use, after passing through the first gate, take a path to Nanmor car park and bear right to the lane. Turn left and, in 100 metres, take another lane on the left. After about 150 metres, you cross the railway line.) Pass a chapel and continue along the lane for another 500 metres to a right bend.

4. Turn left through a small gate at a cattle grid onto an access lane. Pass some houses and walk uphill around several bends until you reach the end of the lane. (Be sure to look back at the views.) Go through a gate into a yard and leave it by the opposite gate. Walk along the left side of the field, passing below the house (Carneddi) and, in 50 metres, pass through a kissing-gate on the left. Follow the left side of the field to a field gate and continue ahead, slightly right, to a tree covered hummock. Bear right, downhill, on a winding path to a field.

The path goes ahead for a few metres then bends to the left and, further on, goes through a gap in a wall. Continue ahead and, when the track veers slightly right to descend more steeply, bear left on a path to a small gate.

5. Continue beside a fence through the woodlands and ignore a path on the right. Walk uphill and pass through a gap in a wall then follow the winding path through moss covered boulders. After a level stretch, the path descends and passes behind a house. Further on, you will pass another house on your left. Follow its access drive for about 10 metres, then leave it to go ahead through a field to a stile. The path continues through bracken and soon has the Nanmor stream on its right. Cross a stream and bear right to a ladder stile and lane.

6. Turn left along the lane for just over a kilometre and, at a cottage on the left, bear left to have the garden wall on your right. Go through a gate and follow the clear path ahead to have great views of Yr Wyddfa (Snowdon). The path goes uphill, then descends steeply to a dip. Go over a lower hill and climb a ladder stile in the right-hand wall. Follow the wall on your left and cross a track then walk up to a stile near the trees at Coed Llywelyn. Further on, cross a stream and walk ahead to a house (Hafod Owen). Pass through a gap to climb a stile and pass the house on your left. Follow the path through rhododendrons and descend the steps of a stile.

7. Walk through an area of cut rhododendrons and follow the path to a ladder stile. The path is quite clear and has way marks in places as it winds around crags and over a stile into trees. Pass above a ruin and bear right to pass it on your right. Climb a stile to leave the woods and turn left.

8. Ignore a path on the right and walk uphill to pass ruins on your left. Go over the rise and downhill to the lakeside at Llyn Dinas. Bear left over a stile, ford Afon Goch and, at the end of the lake, go through a kissing-gate. Ignore the footbridge on

your right and follow the clear path through gates until you meet a track. Turn left and pass the car park entrance for Sygun Mine on your left. After going through a gap in a wall, turn right on a path beside the wall and follow it until you meet another track.

9. Turn right and go through the gate onto a lane. Follow the lane for just over a kilometre and, when it bends right at a bridge, climb a stile on the left. Follow the path beside the river, then over a lane and along another path to the footbridge over Afon Glaslyn in Beddgelert.

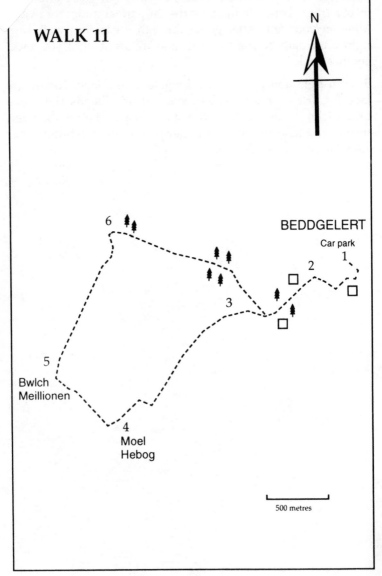

WALK 11

N

BEDDGELERT

Car park

1

2

6

3

5

Bwlch
Meillionen

4

Moel
Hebog

500 metres

Walk 11   *4.5 or 6.5 miles/7 or 9.5 kilometres*

Moel Hebog

Start:	Beddgelert. Main car park off the A498.
Time:	4 hours to the summit and back by its outward route. 5 hours for the circular walk.
Grade:	Strenuous.
Terrain:	Hill paths with rough, rocky sections. The longer walk takes in forest paths and tracks with open views.

Moel Hebog (*moel:* barren hill; *hebog:* hawk) is Beddgelert's own mountain. The ascent requires some strenuous walking but the wide panoramic views make the effort worthwhile. From the summit, on clear days, are stunning views of the Llŷn peninsula and Snowdonia's peaks, encompassing the Nantlle and Yr Wyddfa ridges, Yr Aran, Moel Siabod, Y Cnicht and the Moelwynion.

Owain Glyndŵr is said to have climbed the precipitous gully known as Simnai y Foel (see Walk 8). Successfully evading capture, he hid in a cave on Moel yr Ogof's east face.

An aircraft crashed on the mountain on 13 June 1944 on a night navigation exercise and there was one survivor. Avro Anson EG472 had been flying low because one of the crew was feeling sick from air turbulence but there was trouble with the radios. Sergeant Harry Howard had just taken off his harness when the Anson struck Moel Hebog, and he was thrown through the fabric roof of the aircraft. He rolled downhill until stopped by a rock, then, bruised and dazed, he started to crawl down the steep slope. Meanwhile, the aircraft had carried on, only to burst into flames as it hit cliffs higher up the mountain. A farmer at Cwm Cloch had heard the aircraft fly overhead and seen the blaze when it crashed. The RAF Mountain Rescue was notified and, after they set up base at the farm, the farmer guided the rescue team up Moel Hebog. They found Howard about one hour later, around 4.00 a.m., but the four other members of the crew had died in the crash. Sergeant Howard, who was from Wigan, soon recovered from his injuries and married a girl who lived in Caernarfon.

Walk Directions:

1. From the car park walk out to the road and turn right. In a few paces, turn right to pass the Royal Goat Hotel on your left. When the road turns left, veer right on a track and, in a few metres, bear left on a path. Cross the road at houses, and continue ahead to cross a bridge over the Welsh Highland Railway track. Turn right on a grassy track between walls and follow it when it bears left above a stream to a ladder stile.

2. Cross a bridge and turn left along a track to pass farm buildings on your right. Walk through a pine wood and, at the next farmhouse, Cwm Gloch Ganol, cross a stile on your right near a barn. Follow the clear path ahead through a flat area and, after a footbridge, climb a stile at some enclosures.

3. The path veers left to climb the north-east ridge. Pass through a gap in a wall and, higher up, climb a stile at a small gate. Continue up the ridge, enjoying the backward views, with the cliffs of Y Diffwys to your right. The path becomes steeper as it veers right over rocks and scree to reach the top of the ridge. Bear left to Moel Hebog's summit and trig. point.

4. For the shorter walk, retrace your steps to the start. The longer, circular walk follows the wall that goes north from the summit in the direction of Moel Lefn. It descends to a col, Bwlch Meillionen, the lowest point in the ridge between Moel Hebog and Moel yr Ogof. After crossing a low wall, join the path that crosses the pass from Cwm Pennant. Bear right beside

the wall and, lower down, with Owain Glyndŵr's cave high above you, go through a gap to descend the steep slope to a stile at the edge of the forest.

5. Follow the path downhill and cross a forest track. The path descends through heather and felled forest. After crossing three more forest tracks, and a stream, at the next track turn left and, after a bridge, bear right downhill to a wider track.

6. Turn right and follow the track above Meillionen Farm. Ignore a right fork and, where the track bends left, bear right on a path to a stile and stream. After going through a gate, follow the path through trees and over a channel to another small gate. The path continues over rough ground beside the wall, then bears right through a gate to rejoin your outward route near the barn at Cwm Cloch Ganol.

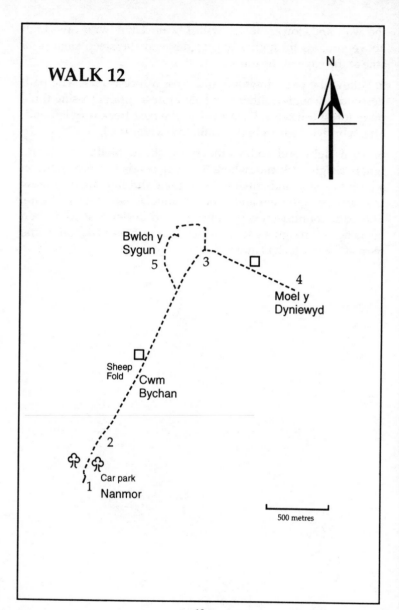

WALK 12

N

Bwlch y
Sygun

5   3

4
Moel y
Dyniewyd

Sheep
Fold

Cwm
Bychan

2

Car park

1

Nanmor

500 metres

Moel y Dyniewyd

Start: Nanmor. Car park off the A4085 near Pont Aberglaslyn.

Time: 3 hours.

Grade: Moderate/Strenuous.

Terrain: Woodland and moorland paths. Steep climb over heather and rock from the pass to the summit of Moel y Dyniewyd.

Moel y Dyniewyd is the highest summit of the rugged hills lying between Nantgwynant and Nanmor. Although only a modest 1254 feet (382 metres) high, this little mountain offers spectacular, panoramic views that take in Yr Wyddfa *(Snowdon)*, Moel Hebog, Arddu and Y Cnicht.

On your walk up Cwm Bychan, you will pass remains of old copper mines. A processing plant was sited near the Welsh Highland Railway line and here you may notice two circular, concrete buddles. Higher up the valley are the pylons of an overhead ropeway that transported ore to the plant. The busiest time for these mines was at the end of the 18th century and they were worked occasionally until 1930.

The walk also passes the Llyndu mine. Worked during the first half of the 19th century, the ore yielded up to 30% of copper. The remains include a paved area where twenty girls worked at separating the ore from the rock.

Walk Directions:

1. From the car park, go through a small gate near the toilet block and turn right under the Welsh Highland Railway bridge. Bear left uphill to a higher path and turn right. The path passes

through some woodland and, just before a gate, you will see a small waterfall.

2. Continue along the path uphill through Cwm Bychan and, after crossing a stream, pass a sheepfold on your left and further on, spoil heaps and pylons. After the last pylon, ignore paths on the left and follow the path uphill to the gap in the hills ahead.

3. Climb a stile and, after a few paces, bear right on a narrow path that wanders through heather with a fence nearby on the right. There are several ups and downs and you will pass a small marshy pool in a dip, after which the path becomes rockier and steeper. Stay as near to the fence as you can and, higher up, climb a stile in it. Walk on up the ridge with the fence now on your left and, after a few minutes, you will reach Moel y Dyniewyd's summit cairn.

4. It is safest to return the way you came to the pass – this little mountain has steep cliffs on the south and east sides. A small variation from the pass can be made by turning right (instead of left over the stile) and following the path downhill for about 100 metres to a footpath signpost. Bear left to pass the remains of the Llyndu copper mine and climb a ladder stile. The path goes left beside the fence for about 30 metres then bears right and descends through crags to join another path.

5. Turn left and after 300 metres you will rejoin your outward route in Cwm Bychan. Turn right to retrace your steps to the car park at Nanmor.

Llyn Dinas

Start: Llyn Dinas. Car park on the A498 near the western
                 end of the lake.

Time: 2-3 hours.

Grade: Easy/Moderate.

Terrain: Hillside and lakeside paths, tracks, lane.

After following the lakeside path for a short distance, the walk climbs to moorland from where there are great views of Llyn Dinas and the surrounding mountains.

Llyn Dinas is a fairly shallow lake, having a maximum depth of 30 feet. In the 1950s the lower end of the lake was used by Twentieth Century Fox for a sequence in the film 'The Inn of the Sixth Happiness'. The film was based on the book 'The Small Woman' by Anthony Burgess which tells the true story of Gladys Aylward, a missionary in China. Ingrid Bergman acted the part of the main character. In the film, while fleeing from the Japanese, she and her schoolchildren arrive at a river (Llyn Dinas) and, from near the boathouse, they crossed the lake on a makeshift raft to the opposite side.

The piece of land between the lake, Afon Glaslyn and the road was used in the past as a pen for stray goats. On the first day of May each year, it was the custom to cover a large raft with turf and branches to symbolise earth. From the upper end of the lake, with a man and woman on board, the boat was towed the length of the lake by two oxen. The beasts were then slaughtered as a sacrifice on a small hill overlooking Afon Glaslyn, where a huge bonfire was lit.

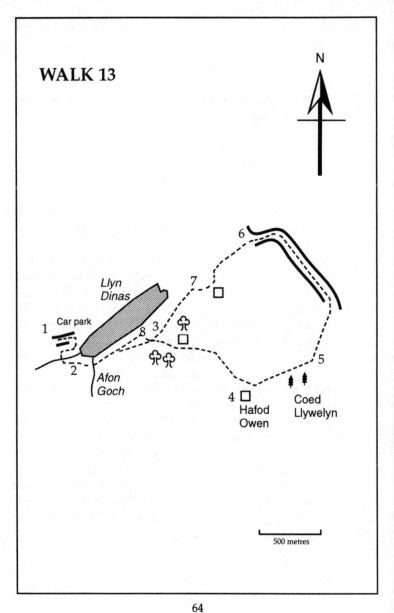

WALK 13

N

Llyn
Dinas

Car park

1

2

Afon
Goch

8 3

7

6

5

4 Hafod
Owen

Coed
Llywelyn

500 metres

Walk Directions:

1. With your back to the parking area turn left and, in a few paces, go through a kissing-gate on the right. Follow the path to a footbridge and, after crossing Afon Glaslyn, bear left through a kissing-gate.

2. Ignore a path on the right that ascends the hillside and walk ahead on the lakeside path. After crossing Afon Goch and climbing a ladder stile, you will reach a fork in the path. Take the right-hand fork to go over a small, rocky hill and walk downhill to a stile. Ignore a path on the left and, after 50 metres, cross a ladder stile on your right.

3. Pass ruins on your left and, after 30 metres, bear left above the ruins. After crossing another stile, ignore a rising path on your right and descend a rocky path that gradually rises to a wall. Further on, go through a gap and follow the path to a stile. Pass through an area of cut rhododendrons and climb a ladder stile near a stream.

4. Walk uphill through the rhododendrons to a house called Hafod Owen and pass it on your right. Climb a stile and go right through a gap then left to have a wall on your left. Cross some streams and climb a stile near the coniferous plantation, Coed Llywelyn. With the wall nearby on your right, walk downhill to join a track at a gate on your right.

5. Turn left on the broad track and walk downhill. Climb a ladder stile and, further on, emerge through a gate onto a lane. Bear left downhill and, after about 900 metres, at a right-hand bend, bear left through a gate at a cattle grid.

6. Walk ahead along the track to pass a barn and, further on, a house on the left, then go over a bridge and climb a ladder stile near a gate. Cross a bridge over a stream and, almost immediately, veer right, with a fence nearby on your right to a ladder stile.

7. Continue on a clear path, between outcrops, to another stile. Take the path through a marshy area and continue along the woodland edge. Climb a stile and, in another 250 metres, you will pass a stile on the left that you crossed earlier in the walk. In another 50 metres, bear right on a path that leads to a ladder stile near Llyn Dinas.

8. The rocky path passes close to the lakeside and rejoins your outward route at the next stile. Ford Afon Goch and cross the footbridge over Afon Glaslyn to return to the car park.

Craflwyn, Bethania and Llyn Dinas

Start:	Llyn Dinas. Car park on the A498 near the western end of the lake.
Time:	4 hours.
Grade:	Moderate.
Terrain:	Hill and lakeside paths.

After leaving the valley, this walk climbs gentle hill paths through National Trust owned land to Afon Cwm Llan and its fine waterfalls. The return route is on easy level paths by Llyn Dinas.

Llywelyn ap Iorwerth gave these lands to the monks of Aberconwy Abbey in 1198. After the dissolution of the monasteries, the property passed into the hands of the Wynn family of Gwydir, and tenant farmers worked the land. Craflwyn dates back to the 16th century when it was the finest mansion in the valley. In the 17th century, it was the home of Humphrey Jones, Receiver General of northern Wales. Llywelyn England Sydney Parry inherited the Craflwyn estate in 1873 and built the present Craflwyn Hall. As was usual in the Victorian era, he laid out formal gardens with fishponds and planted exotic trees and rhododendrons.

When the National Trust took over the property in 1994, one of the major tasks was to remove most of the rhododendrons from the land. Although pretty to look at when in bloom rhododendron is an alien species and, as it spreads quickly, prevents the growth of native plants. Craflwyn Hall is now a residential centre for conservation volunteers.

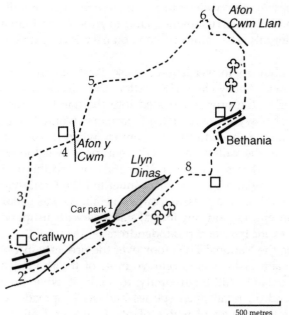

WALK 14

N

Afon Cwm Llan

6

5

☐
4

Afon y Cwm

Llyn Dinas

Car park 1

3

☐ Craflwyn

2

7 ☐

Bethania

8 ☐

500 metres

Walk Directions:

1. With your back to the car park, bear left for a few metres then go through a kissing-gate on the right. Walk beside Llyn Dinas and cross a footbridge where Afon Glaslyn leaves the lake. Turn right on a path and go through a small gate. Pass below a house and go through another gate to reach a track. Turn right over a bridge and, immediately, bear left through a small gate. Follow the path over little footbridges until it emerges on the road.

2. Cross the road to the entrance gates for Craflwyn Hall. Follow the drive and bear left then take a track on the right. Walk uphill to pass between buildings and the back of Craflwyn Hall. Go through a gate and, in about 50 metres, bear left on a grassy track beside a wall. Go through a gate and walk uphill to meet another path.

3. Turn right and follow the path that is way marked with red arrows. It passes through an area of cleared rhododendrons and, higher up, you will see a seat on your right from where there is a great view of Dinas Emrys (see Walk 6). Continue uphill along the path and climb a small stile over a fence. The path bears to the left and you will soon reach a path junction. Turn right (there may be a Hafod y Llan sign and a black arrow) and follow the path to a footbridge and stile. The path continues through rough pasture and, further on, you will pass a ruined barn on your left.

4. Climb a ladder stile in the right-hand fence and use the stepping-stones to cross Afon y Cwm. Join a track and bear left to cross another stile. Follow the track to a building at old copper mine workings. Ignore a little path on the right and take the path past the building and around to the right. You will pass a 'Mine Danger' notice and piles of spoil.

5. The path crosses a stream and winds gently upwards through heather and outcrops to the highest part of the walk.

Enjoy your last views westwards and walk downhill to a ladder stile in a wall. Follow the way marks through a fairly flat area and, further on, join a clearer path. After passing a crag, have a wall on your right and, further downhill, climb a stile in it. Take the clear path downhill, with views towards Yr Wyddfa *(Snowdon)*. Ignore the gate ahead and go slightly right to join the Watkin Path.

6. Turn right downhill, following the bends, and you will soon have fine views of Afon Cwm Llan waterfalls. Go through a gate across the track to a fork and bear right. Follow the path over footbridges until you emerge near a lane and the main road.

7. Turn right along the road for 300 metres then turn left on a lane. After 200 metres, where the lane bends left, bear right through a gate at a cattle grid. Follow the track to pass a barn and a house on the left. After crossing a bridge, pass a building on the left and climb a stile at a gate. Cross another bridge and bear right near a fence to a ladder stile.

8. Continue on a path beside outcrops and, after another stile, walk through a marshy area. Pass beside woodlands and climb a stile, but ignore a stile on the left into the woods. Ignore a path on the right and walk uphill to climb a stile and pass ruins on the left. Go over a rise and downhill to Llyn Dinas, where you bear left over a ladder stile and ford Afon Goch. At the end of the lake, go through a kissing-gate and bear right over the footbridge to retrace your steps to the start.

Cwm Llan

Start: Pont Bethania. Car park on the A498 between Llyn Dinas and Llyn Gwynant.

Time: 3 hours.

Grade: Moderate.

Terrain: Steady climb at the start of the walk. The walk takes in hill, woodland and riverside paths.

Cwm Llan makes a fine destination for those who do not want to walk all the way to the summit of Yr Wyddfa *(Snowdon)*. This half-day walk on the Watkin Path, passing the impressive waterfalls of Afon Cwm Llan, should not be missed. The route goes through land belonging to Hafod y Llan farm which was purchased by the National Trust in 1998 following a successful public appeal. The estate's land extends to the summit of Yr Wyddfa.

Early in the walk, you will pass the site of Sir Edward Watkin's chalet. Built in the 1890s on the site of an old cottage, the building had its own supply of electricity powered by Afon Gorsen. Sadly, the chalet was destroyed at the end of the 1939-1945 war after being occupied by the army.

The Watkin Path was built in 1892. Sir Edward Watkin, Liberal MP, brought William Gladstone, who was Prime Minister at that time, to Cwm Llan to open the path for public use for ever. Over 2,000 people gathered around a temporary, wooden platform on a rocky outcrop, the Gladstone Rock, to hear his speech on 13 September 1892. Several Welsh choirs were present and Mr Gladstone much enjoyed the hymns.

As you follow the track uphill past the waterfalls you will go through a cutting that was part of a tramway for the Hafod y

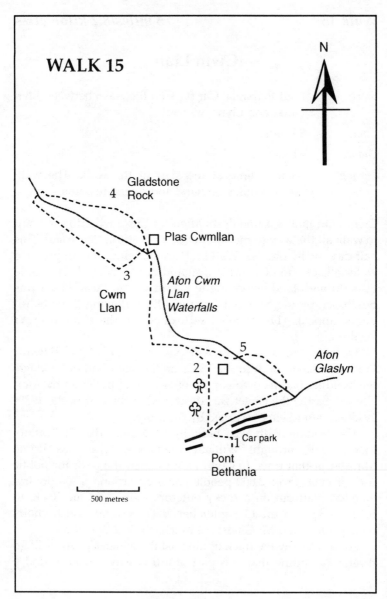

WALK 15

N

Gladstone
4   Rock

□ Plas Cwmllan

3

Cwm
Llan

*Afon Cwm
Llan
Waterfalls*

5

*Afon
Glaslyn*

2   □

Car park
1

Pont
Bethania

500 metres

Llan (Snowdon) quarry. It ended at the road near Pont Bethania and from there the slates were transported by horse drawn wagons to Porthmadog. In the 1870s there were hopes of a railway line in the valley, but it never arrived.

On the far side of Afon Cwm Llan are old copper workings and the remains of a mill, wheel pits and dressing floors where the copper was crushed before being sold in Liverpool and Swansea. The walk then takes the Braich-yr-Oen copper mine's tramway uphill to meet the level slate mine's tramway, which it follows through cuttings to the derelict buildings of the Hafod y Llan slate quarry. The slate quarry operated from the 1840s to the 1880s. You can see the remains of workshops and dressing sheds. Near the Watkin Path are the barracks where the workers lived during the week, although they went home at the weekends. Between here and the Gladstone Rock, the Watkin Path goes along the slate quarry's original tramway. Just beyond the rock, you will pass Plas Cwmllan, the slate quarry manager's house. It was used for commando training during the 1939-1945 war and bullet holes can still be seen in the walls.

Walk Directions:

1. From the car park, cross the bridge over the river to the main road. Bear left and, in a few metres, turn right on a lane. Immediately, leave the lane to go up steps to a small gate. Follow the path through the wood and, at a track junction, bear left through a gate.

2. Follow the track uphill and, as you rise, Afon Cwm Llan waterfalls come into view. The track goes around left and right bends to reach a gate above the river. Continue along the path until it stops rising then bear left on the path that was the Braich-yr-Oen tramway.

3. The path goes uphill to meet a level tramway. Turn right along it and, at the slate quarry's ruined buildings, cross a bridge over the river. Bear right on a path to join the Watkin

Path just below the slate quarry's barracks. Turn right and you will soon see the Gladstone Rock with its plaque on your right.

4. Further on along the track, you will pass the derelict Plas Cwmllan. Cross the bridge over Afon Cwm Llan and follow the Watkin Path downhill for about one kilometre. Just after the right bend, look for a path on the left descending towards the river. Follow it downhill to a gate on top of a wall, and, further downhill, turn left through a gate. Bear right to walk through a camping field and, after passing through a gate, turn left over a bridge.

5. Walk through a long field and bear right on a track through a gap in a wall. After a few more metres, slant right across the field and go through a gap to a footbridge. Bear left and follow the path beside Afon Glaslyn to a footbridge and lane. Turn left through a gate at a cattle grid to the A498 and car park.

Llyn Gwynant

Start: Pont Bethania. Car park on the A498 between Llyn
             Dinas and Llyn Gwynant.

Time: 4 hours.

Grade: Moderate.

Terrain: Field, hillside and forest paths, lane. Care needed
             in places on the path above Llyn Gwynant.

This lovely, varied walk takes you to a rocky viewpoint above
Llyn Gwynant.

According to local legend, Prince Madog, who may have
discovered America long before Christopher Columbus, lived
in this valley. He was one of the sons of Owain Gwynedd and,
after Owain died in 1169, Madog's older brothers Dafydd and
Hywel battled against each other to rule Gwynedd. Peace
loving Prince Madog did not wish to take sides and, being a
proven sailor, he set sail in the Gwennan Gorn, a ship built of
oak from the Nant Gwynant forests. After discovering new land
in the west, where he left most of his men, he returned to Wales
to find emigrants and persuaded enough men and women to
fill ten ships. They sailed with him to the newly discovered
land, now thought to be Alabama.

In the 1830s, an exorcist from Pwllheli banished a poltergeist
to the bottom of Llyn Gwynant after it caused havoc at Hafod
Llwyfog. Apart from throwing things about, the ghost had a
habit of lifting the servants' beds and letting them drop with a
clang. It once squeezed a servant's leg so much that he could
not move for two weeks.

At about the same time, Plas Gwynant was also reputed to
be haunted. The estate had been sold in 1803 to Daniel Vawdrey

N

4

Llyn
Gwynant

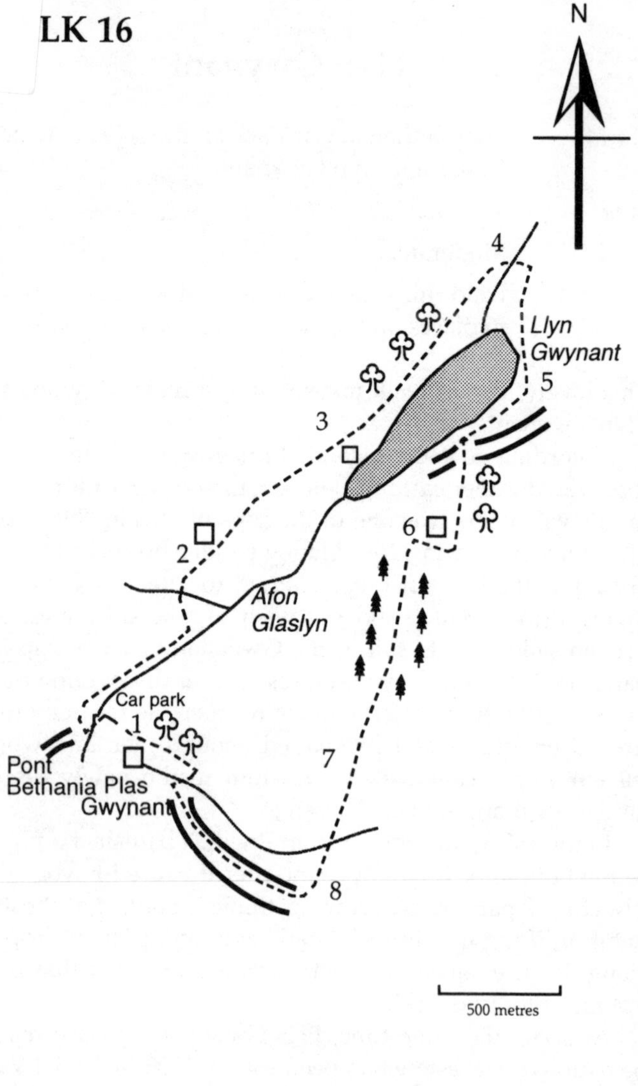

5

3

2

Afon
Glaslyn

6

Car park

1

7

Pont
Bethania Plas
Gwynant

8

500 metres

who improved his lands by planting trees and making roads. The Plas did not stay occupied for long as all those who stayed in it soon moved out because of the weird noises. Mr Vawdrey offered free accommodation at the Plas to a newly married couple who worked for him. All was peaceful for a couple of years, but then a ghostly apparition appeared to the woman and she fainted. She died a few months later. Eventually, another of Vawdrey's servants, Gruffudd ap Rhisiart, stayed at the Plas and, because he refused to be perturbed by the ghost, it soon departed. Sometime later, James Anthony Froude occupied Plas Gwynant and his literary visitors included Tom Hughes and Charles Kingsley. The house is now an outdoor centre. Another old house in the valley called Bryn Gwynant has become a youth hostel.

Walk Directions:

1. From the car park, cross the bridge to the main road. Bear left and, in a few metres, turn right on a lane. Go through a small gate next to a cattle grid and, after about 100 metres, bear right over a footbridge. Continue on a path beside Afon Glaslyn and, after crossing a footbridge over a smaller river, bear left through a gap in a broken wall. Slant to the right across the field to join a track near a wall.

2. Bear right and go through a gap in a wall. Walk ahead and climb a stile near a building then continue near the river. Follow the track as it bears left, away from the river, but at a right bend, go uphill on a path. The path soon swings to the right to have a hill on its right. Go through a gap in a wall and, with woodlands to your left, head uphill on a clear path. Pass a spoil heap and follow the path downhill. It soon veers to the left through a reedy area and passes a ruin on the right.

3. Climb a stile into woodland and cross a bridge over a stream. The path rises through trees and crosses a steep wooded slope – take care – to a rock buttress with fine views over Llyn

Gwynant. Go downhill to a small footbridge and follow the hillside path to a ladder stile in woodlands. Have a wall on your right and walk through an area of massive fallen rocks to a footbridge on your right.

4. After crossing the footbridge, walk ahead for a few metres then bear right through the campsite to a line of trees at the lakeside. Bear left beside the lake and ignore a stile on the left. Climb a stile just above the lake and follow a path over a rise and down to the lake again. Continue beside it until you reach the A498.

5. Turn right and follow a path beside the road for 400 metres. After the road crosses a stream, turn left through a gate onto a track. Follow it for about 100 metres and, when it bends right, go up steps on the left. Walk uphill with a wall on your left to rejoin the track, but soon leave it again, when it bears right, to continue beside the wall. Higher up, join the track again and continue along it. After the wall on your right ends, follow the track when it bends right towards farm buildings.

6. Ignore a path on the right signed 'Youth Hostel Only' and pass a building on your right. Go through a gap in the wall and follow a path that goes left through dense rhododendrons to a wall corner. Bear right and follow a path through the trees to a ladder stile. Continue through tall coniferous trees to a stile at the end of the wood. The path winds through rhododendrons to a small gate in the left-hand wall.

7. The path maintains its direction, but slightly left, and goes uphill through a gap in a wall. From here are fine views towards Snowdon. Keep to the right of a hill and bear right to a footbridge. Turn left to a ladder stile and continue ahead to a lane.

8. Bear right downhill and, after about one kilometre, turn right on a footpath. Cross a footbridge and walk up to a track then turn left. Pass below a house and, after a gate, bear right to the main road and car park.

Around Y Gyrn

Start: Forest car park off the A4085, half-way between
             Beddgelert and Rhyd-ddu.

Time: 3-4 hours.

Grade: Moderate/Strenuous.

Terrain: Forest and moorland paths and tracks. Some paths
             may be very wet in places.

Choose a clear day for this walk so that you can enjoy superb
views of Yr Wyddfa *(Snowdon)*, the Nantlle Ridge and Cwm
Pennant. The walk climbs up through forest and moorland to
Bwlch Cwm Trwsgl, then traverses the upper reaches of Cwm
Pennant to the highest part of the walk, Bwlch y Ddwy Elor
(Pass of the Two Biers), an ancient pass linking the valley with
Rhyd-ddu. Cwm Pennant was the birthplace of poet Eliseus
Williams (Eifion Wyn), a poet who immortalized his feelings for
the valley that was his home with this couplet (translated from
the Welsh):

'O Lord, why did you make Cwm Pennant so beautiful
And the life of an old shepherd so short?'

He died in 1926 at the age of 59.

As you climb up towards Bwlch y Ddwy Elor you will pass
the remains of the Prince of Wales slate quarry. First worked in
the 1860s, its most productive years were between 1873 and
1886 when up to 200 men were employed with an output of
5,000 tons a year. A prominent feature in the valley is the
Gorseddau tramway along which the slate was transported to
Porthmadog. After 1886, the quarry was worked in a small way
until the 1920s.

The last stages of the walk take you through an area once

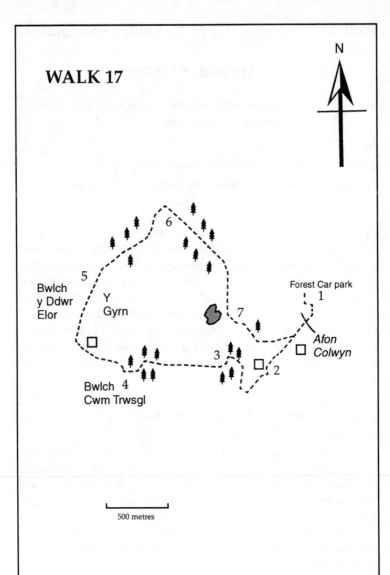

WALK 17

N

Forest Car park
1

Bwlch
y Ddwr
Elor

Y
Gyrn

5

6

7

Afon
Colwyn

3

2

Bwlch
Cwm Trwsgl

4

500 metres

known as the 'Land of the Fairies'. In times past, a midwife used to tell the story of how she was brought from her valley on a grey horse to a sumptuous palace in Cwm Hafod Ruffydd, where she assisted a lady and stayed with her until she recovered. Everybody she met danced and sang all day and night long. When the time came for her to leave, she was presented with a large purse which she was instructed not to open until she arrived at her home. A servant returned her there and, when she opened the purse, she found it contained enough money to live on comfortably for the rest of her life.

There is also another, sadder, story concerning the cwm. At Hafod Ruffydd Ucha, in the early 19th century, there lived a farmer's wife who was a skilled nurse. One day she was asked to help in an emergency at a nearby farm. To get there, she had to cross Afon Hafod Ruffydd, the river that flows from Llyn Llywelyn. It was in spate and, as she crossed, she lost her footing and was carried away by the water and drowned.

Walk Directions:

1. Walk towards the car park entrance and, before the track junction, turn right on a path. Follow it to a bridge and turn right to cross it. Follow the track uphill (crossing the Welsh Highland Railway track) and pass the drive to a house on your left. Continue uphill and ignore a narrower track on the right. Bear left to soon have a wall on your right and at the end of the wall, turn right on an access track for Hafod Ruffydd Uchaf.

2. After approximately 50 metres, bear left on a track to pass around a barrier and walk uphill to a track junction. Turn right for about 200 metres then bear left on a narrow path. Emerge on a track and go ahead on a path that cuts off a bend in the track. Cross it again and continue on the path until it merges on the track again. Turn left for a few paces and, at a yellow way mark, bear right and walk uphill to a stile at the edge of the forest.

3. Follow the path, way marked in places, through rough grass and heather. From here are fine views of the mountain peaks. Cross a stream and go through a gap in a wall then walk downhill through the trees to a track and turn left. Bear right at a way mark and follow a path uphill to a stile on a minor pass called Bwlch Cwm Trwsgl between Moel Lefn and Y Gyrn.

4. Cross to the far side of a wall and bear right downhill with the wall on your right. Continue beside the wall through a marshy area, then go left on a path. You will soon have fine views of the Nantlle ridge. Pass ruined buildings and a fenced mine shaft, then walk uphill on a clear path. Pass another ruin and ignore a level path to the right. Climb a little higher, then turn right and soon pass a stretch of wall on your left. (Ignore paths on the left.) Pass ruins on your left and a quarry to the right then head uphill – be sure to look back at the views down Cwm Pennant. Go slightly left at the top to a gate in the pass of Bwlch y Ddwy Elor.

5. Continue along the path, which soon enters the forest and passes the remains of quarrying. The path becomes broader before emerging on a forest track, where you turn right to a junction. Ignore the track on the left and walk ahead for about another 50 metres, then go left on a path downhill.

6. Emerge at a track crossroads and bear right to another track junction, where you turn left. (Before turning left you may like to take the track to the right for a few metres to a picnic area at Llyn Llywelyn.)

7. Descend the track and cross over another track to continue walking downhill on an old stony track. About 400 metres from this last junction, bear left on a narrow path and follow it to another track. Turn left to the bridge crossed earlier and bear left on a path to retrace your steps to the car park.

Llyn y Gadair

Start: Car park on the A4085, south of the village, near
            the Welsh Highland Railway station.

Time: About 2 hours.

Grade: Moderate.

Terrain: Hill and forest paths and tracks. Some paths are
            unclear and may be wet in places.

Llyn y Gadair is on land traditionally believed to be fairy
territory and, in the olden days, the area was full of the little
folk singing and dancing at every full moon. Marshy valleys
with rivers and lakes surrounded by grassy hills were said to
attract particularly beautiful, joyous and mischievous members
of the Tylwyth Teg.

One night, a young man returning from Beddgelert to his
home at the farm called Fridd near Rhyd-ddu came upon fairies
dancing beside Llyn y Gadair. Fascinated, he stopped to watch
them but fell asleep. The Tylwyth Teg found him and tied him
up then covered his body with gossamer so that he could not be
seen. A search party failed to find him, and he was not released
by the fairies until the following evening. Utterly bewildered,
he wandered about the slopes of Y Gadair until daybreak, when
he realised he was less than a mile from home.

The walk traverses Y Gadair, a low hill south-west of the
lake which, long ago, may have been the site of a bardic centre.
Cwm Marchnad once held markets established at the time of
Edward I. Near the stream are the ruins of an old tavern that
closed in 1815.

You will pass the remains of Llyn y Gadair slate quarry, a
co-operative venture that opened in 1885. The slate was

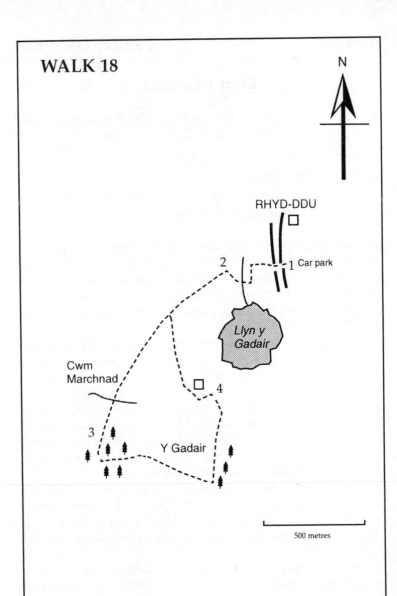

WALK 18

N

RHYD-DDU

1 Car park

Llyn y Gadair

Cwm Marchnad

2

4

3

Y Gadair

500 metres

transported by cart to the railway at Rhyd-ddu. Although a causeway was built for a line to the slate quarry, it was never railed. The quarry ceased operating in the 1920s.

Walk Directions:

1. From the car park, cross the road to a kissing-gate. Follow the paved path through a marshy area and turn left at a stream. Go through a small gate and cross a footbridge to a stile. Cross a drive and follow a path through rough pasture to a track then turn right to a stile near a gate and road.

2. Turn left through a gate with a bridleway sign and follow a wall to a small gate. Ignore a track on the left and, further on, a path on the right. Walk uphill to a stile and follow a clear path that is way marked with white arrows painted on rocks. The path goes through a gate and crosses a few streams before entering the forest through a bridle gate.

3. Walk ahead through the forest to a track crossroads and turn left. From this track are fine views of the surrounding mountains. After following the track for about one kilometre, at a point where the track bends right, look for a narrow path on the left. Walk through the trees and cross a stile. Turn right to follow a fence and cross a broken wall into the forest. Keep the wall on your left and go over a slight rise to have views of Llyn y Gadair. Descend beside the wall to mine buildings.

4. On reaching the mine workings, immediately bear left. Pass a low ruin and climb a stile on your right, behind the ruin. Bear right a few paces to cross a stream and walk in the direction of a distant farm. Pass a quarry pool on your right and other ruins. Go through a break in a wall and cross a stream to have a fenced off field to your right. Proceed uphill and cross another stream to arrive at two gates. Take the left-hand gate and continue ahead with a fence on your right. After following it for about 100 metres, you will rejoin your outward route at a ladder stile. Turn right to retrace your steps to the car park.

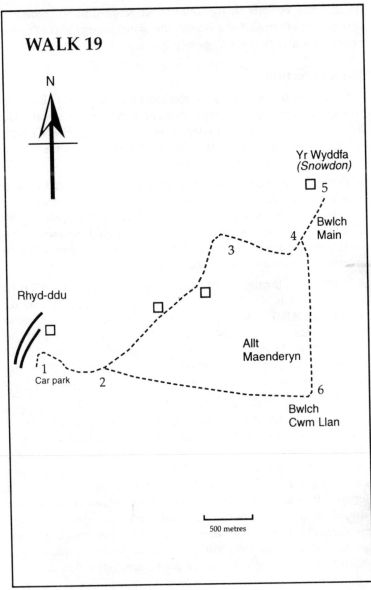

WALK 19

N

Yr Wyddfa
(Snowdon)
☐ 5

Bwlch
4 Main

3

Rhyd-ddu

☐

Allt
Maenderyn

1
Car park
2
6
Bwlch
Cwm Llan

500 metres

Yr Wyddfa (*Snowdon*)

Start: Rhyd-ddu. Car park south of the village on the A4085, near the Welsh Highland Railway station.

Time: 5-6 hours.

Grade: Strenuous.

Terrain: Rough mountain paths. The upper section follows a narrow ridge (avoid in high winds).

The Rhyd-ddu path is one of the easier and less well used routes up Yr Wyddfa. In clear weather the walk offers magnificent, panoramic views. At one time, it was called the Beddgelert Path and there is an alternative start at Pitt's Head (but no parking) nearer Beddgelert. Higher stretches of the path should be avoided in strong winds and when the ground is covered in snow or ice.

Early in the walk, you will pass on your left a small, round tower that used to be the powder house for the Ffrith slate quarry which closed in the 1860s. The workings of the quarry are passed a little further on. After joining the path from Pitt's Head, the route bears left and climbs gradually to the ruins of a small hut where, many years ago, an old woman and her son made refreshments for walkers.

The path becomes steeper as it climbs to the Llechog ridge where you are rewarded with fine views into Cwm Clogwm with its three small lakes. This is Tylwyth Teg country and long ago, it is said, fairies used to sing and dance around Llyn Coch, the middle lake. A young shepherd fell in love with one of them and he was allowed to marry her on condition he never struck her with iron. They had children but, one day, he accidentally hit her with a bridle made of iron. Immediately, she vanished into the lake and was never seen again.

Continuing on the path, you will reach the beginning of Bwlch Main. This narrow ridge is quite safe provided walkers take care and keep to the path. This was a popular route in the early 19th century, although many tourists found it scary. Rev. William Bingley crossed the ridge without fear when accompanied by Snowdon guide William Lloyd of Beddgelert, but he states that he would not like to cross it at night. He was told that other travellers, after being guided across the ridge in darkness, were so terrified at seeing it in the morning, they could not return the same way. One man had crawled back over it on his hands and knees.

After reaching broader ground, the route joins the Watkin's Path and soon arrives at the summit where, hopefully, you will be rewarded with panoramic views which, on exceptionally clear days, extend as far as Ireland and the Lake District. Whatever the visibility, you are standing on the highest patch of ground in Wales and England – the height of Yr Wyddfa is 3560 feet. The English translation of Yr Wyddfa is the burial ground and, before the buildings were built, a huge cairn that stood on the summit was said to be the grave of a giant called Rhita Fawr. He killed kings and clothed himself in their beards until one day, King Arthur killed him.

William Lloyd of Beddgelert built the first shelter on the summit around 1815, and about twenty years later, a miner called Williams started serving refreshments in a small hut. A few years after this, the owners of the Royal Hotel in Llanberis built a collection of huts on the summit where visitors could obtain hot meals and alcohol, and stay overnight, often in overcrowded conditions. More huts were built after the coming of the Snowdon Mountain Railway and the building designed by Sir Clough William Ellis (of Portmeirion) was completed in 1935. Plans are now underway for a new, modern building.

Walk Directions:

1. From the car park, pass the toilets on your left and, in about 100 metres, bear right across the railway. Continue on a track and, when it divides, ignore the left-hand fork to Ffridd Isaf farm and take the right-hand track. It climbs gradually to pass the abandoned Ffridd slate quarry. Continue climbing, crossing stiles, until you reach a path junction. Ahead, the path climbs to Bwlch Cwm Llan while the right-hand path comes from Ffridd Uchaf farm.

2. Turn left to go through a kissing-gate and cross a stream. The path goes through a boggy area and heather then crosses a stile. It becomes steeper and, higher up, passes a ruin that was once a half-way hut where walkers could obtain refreshments. After a kissing-gate in a wall the path climbs the shoulder of Llechog and swings right to another kissing-gate.

3. Pause to enjoy the views of Cwm Clogwyn and its lakes then continue along the ridge. A steep section has been fenced to prevent erosion and here the path follows a zig-zag route. After passing a scree slope the path reaches the ridge of Bwlch Main.

4. From Bwlch Main there are great views into Cwm Tregalan and towards Y Lliwedd. The path now bears left to follow the narrow ridge on its right side. You soon reach broader ground and pass the standing stone which marks the path to Bwlch Saethau. It is now only a few minutes walk to the summit of Yr Wyddfa.

5. On leaving the summit, retrace your steps past the marker stone and along Bwlch Main. Ignore the right fork to Rhyd-ddu and take the left-hand path along the south ridge to a stile in a fence. The path continues over Allt Maenderyn and then descends to a wall in the pass of Bwlch y Llan.

6. Turn right and cross the wall to follow the path through the abandoned slate quarries. It bears slightly right and becomes broader as it descends to the junction met earlier, from where you retrace your steps to the start of the walk.

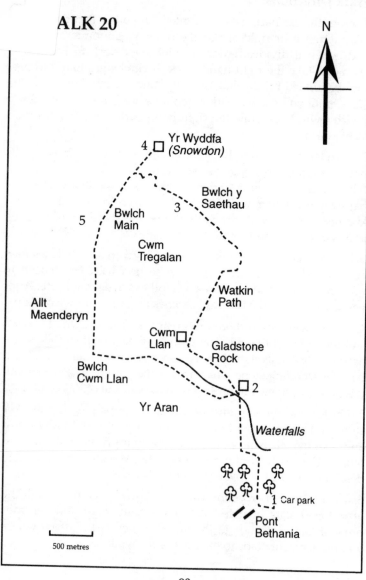

22 Ag 2010

Yr Wyddfa (*Snowdon*)

Start: Pont Bethania. Car park on the A498 between Llyn Dinas and Llyn Gwynant.

Time: 6-7 hours.

Grade: Strenuous.

Terrain: Steep mountain paths. The upper section of the Watkin Path involves a long section of shaly scree.

The Watkin Path is one of the most varied, interesting routes to the summit of Yr Wyddfa (*Snowdon*) but, as it starts at the lowest level of all the paths, it is considered the hardest. The upper scree section is not recommended for children and, in winter and early spring, should only be attempted by experienced mountain walkers, equipped for the conditions likely to be met. Sir Edward Watkin, MP, built the path in the early 1890s so that his guests could reach the summit of Snowdon.

The route starts with an easy, wooded section, passing the site of Edward Watkin's chalet (see Walk 15 to read about the historical features of the first part of the walk). You soon enter open country with views of Afon Cwm Llan waterfalls, and the path climbs past the slate quarry's tramway cutting and old copper mine workings. Soon after the path levels, you pass the ruinous Plas Cwmllan, the home of the former slate quarry manager. It was used for training commandos in the Second World War (there are bullet holes in the walls). After a few hundred metres more, you will see a plaque on a rock commemorating the spot where Prime Minister William Gladstone on 13 September 1892 addressed a huge crowd about 'Justice to Wales'.

At the Hafod y Llan slate quarries, which operated 1840-1882, the path steepens and begins its long haul across the mountainside. Edward Watkin's original path was used by carriages as far as the quarry, and from there his guests rode on donkeys to Bwlch y Saethau. On reaching the ridge at Bwlch Cilau, you can enjoy views stretching to Moel Hebog and the Glaslyn estuary. Down in Cwm Tregalan are the lateral moraines left by the last Ice Age.

According to legend, there was once a city in Cwm Tregalan. King Arthur's enemies, the Saxons, camped in this cwm and, after hearing about it, King Arthur gathered his forces on level ground below Dinas Emrys and marched to Cwm Llan. After hours of fighting, he forced the Saxons up the rocky hillside to the pass. At Bwlch y Saethau (*Pass of the Arrows*), the enemy let fly a last shower of arrows, fatally wounding King Arthur. He sent Sir Bedivere to throw his sword Excalibur into Llyn Glaslyn, and it was on his third attempt that a hand rose from the lake to take the sword. Arthur was carried to Llyn Llydaw, where a boat with three beautiful maidens dressed in white waited and took the dying king into the darkness of the night. Bedivere and the other knights who had survived climbed up to a cave in the precipitous face of Lliwedd, where they still sleep awaiting the return of King Arthur.

From Bwlch y Saethau and its glorious views of the lakes and Grib Goch ridge is the hardest part of the walk, a 900 feet climb up scree to the ridge and the Rhyd-ddu path which you then follow to the summit of Yr Wyddfa.

To return to the start of the walk, you may return by the Watkin Path or follow the circular walk. Alternatively, if it is summer, by making use of the Sherpa bus service, you can descend the mountain by one of the other footpaths and catch a bus back to Pont Bethania.

Walk Directions:

1. From the car park, cross the bridge over the river and bear left along the main road. In a few paces, cross the road to a lane and go up steps to a small gate with a plaque for the Watkin Path. Follow the path through woodlands. On reaching a path on the right, bear left through a gate. The track now enters open countryside and winds to the left, then the right, with views of Afon Cwm Llan waterfalls. The track steepens and becomes more rocky before levelling out just before a bridge.

2. Pass Plas Cwmllan on your right and, further on, you will see the Gladstone Rock to your left. The path steepens again on reaching the ruined buildings of Hafod y Llan slate quarry. Here you veer right on a long steady climb to Bwlch Ciliau. Enjoy the views, which stretch as far as the Glaslyn estuary, and bear left along the north side of Cwm Tregalan to Bwlch y Saethau. Walk across to the edge for views of the Grib Coch ridge and the lakes Llyn Glaslyn and Llyn Llydaw.

3. You are now faced with the hardest part of the climb. The path slants to the left and zig-zags up loose scree to emerge on the south ridge near a tall stone that marks the junction with the Rhyd-ddu path. Turn right to the summit of Snowdon.

4. From the summit retrace your steps to the marker stone but, instead of bearing left down the Watkin Path, follow the Rhyd-ddu path along the exhilarating narrow arete of Bwlch Main.

5. Watch out for a fork where the Rhyd-ddu path bears right. Take the left-hand path that makes a gentle ascent and follows the south ridge. It crosses a stile and soon descends to a wall in the col Bwlch y Llan between Snowdon and Yr Aran. Turn left on a path that descends over stony then wet ground to the old slate quarry tramway in Cwm Llan. Bear right along it and take a steep path (the copper mine tramway) on the left downhill to join the Watkin Path near Plas Cwmllan. From here, retrace your steps to the car park.